# Raising Rover

## Positive Pet Parenting Solutions for your Pooch

**Jodi Schneider McNamee**

authorHOUSE®

*AuthorHouse™*
*1663 Liberty Drive*
*Bloomington, IN 47403*
*www.authorhouse.com*
*Phone: 1 (800) 839-8640*

*Published by AuthorHouse 12/14/2015*

*ISBN: 978-1-5049-6633-7 (sc)*
*ISBN: 978-1-5049-6637-5 (hc)*
*ISBN: 978-1-5049-6634-4 (e)*

*Library of Congress Control Number: 2015920103*

*Print information available on the last page.*

*Cover image: Jodi Schneider McNamee*
*Interior chapter images: Jodi Schneider McNamee*

*This book is printed on acid-free paper.*

# Contents

## SPECIAL SECTION
### Pet Tales to warm the heart

# Acknowledgements

Thank you to the following individuals who without their contributions and support this book would not have been written:

Thanks to Kiki Dolson, publisher of *The Nugget Newspaper* for always thinking of me when animal stories came your way!

Thanks to Jim Cornelius, editor of *The Nugget*, for believing in me as a writer, and for giving me the opportunity to create my Paw Prints pet column!

And to the rest of *The Nugget* staff who have always been so gracious.

Thanks to Jeanie Ogden for allowing me to photograph your beautiful black Lab, Jay Jay, for the book cover!

Thanks to Toni Grinder for bringing your adorable son Corbin out to Sisters multiple times to sit with Jay Jay during photo shoots.

Special thanks to every person I ever interviewed and photographed with their pet for an article in *The Nugget*. Couldn't have done it without your true animal tales!

Special thanks to Eleanor Simonsen, whom I adore like a mom, for your editorial work!

# Introduction

**"Petting, scratching, and cuddling a dog could be as soothing to the mind and heart as deep meditation and almost as food for the soul as prayer" – Dean Koontz**

I don't recall much about when I was four years old, but I distinctly remember my very first family dog. It was 1958 and we lived in the rural countryside of New Jersey. Our backyard was a forest that stretched into acres of red oaks, maples and dogwood that led down a path to a small pond. I would search for pollywogs and salamanders accompanied by Suzie, my huge black standard Poodle. I say huge, because to a four-year-old she seemed the size of a pony. That special forest became our secret garden. I was one with nature. And that's where my compassion for animals began.

Imagine what our lives would be like without our pets, who bless our lives with unconditional love and fill our days with humor, joy and sometimes little spills that keep us busy.

Any pet parent can tell you: pets are amazing. They're loyal, comfort us in tough times, and even lower a person's blood pressure.

At some point in ancient history we developed close relationships with four-legged creatures that would have otherwise been wild, fierce wolves.

Dogs are so in tune with humans that they can tell if their companions are happy or angry. That close relationship has existed since before they helped early humans take down mammoths. But exactly how long canines have provided companionship just got a revision: Instead of pinning domestication at about 11,000 to 16,000 years ago, new genetic evidence shows that man's best friend may have split from wolves 27,000 to 40,000 years ago!

Dogs are such a part of my life that I can't imagine being without them. I appreciate the animal mind and learn something new about the incredible canine every day. I have three rescue dogs, and have to maintain control not to overpopulate my household with more. It isn't easy, because being surrounded by unlimited love 24/7 feels great!

Dogs are remarkably similar to human infants in the way they pay attention to us. This ability accounts for the extraordinary communication we have with our dogs.

Communicating with your furry friend is something so crucial that I have decided to share a wealth of information in *Raising Rover: Positive Pet Parenting Solutions for your Pooch* for anyone who desires to form a unique bond with their dog.

No one said raising Rover is always easy, but knowing how and where to find the type of dog that will fit into your life and how to prepare yourself and your home for him will lighten the load.

When I first began writing for *The Nugget*, the weekly newspaper in Sisters, Oregon, I had no idea that my articles would end up with such a huge focus on animal stories. My adoration for these remarkable creatures showed through. Those articles became a bridge to a weekly pet column that the locals revel in reading, or so I've been told.

Everything I have learned, I have shared in *Raising Rover: Positive Pet Parenting Solutions for your Pooch*, so you can have the best possible relationship with your furry friend.

Whether you're a first-time dog pet parent or an expert, your furry family member would want you to read this book.

I have also added a special section, True Pet Tales to Warm the Heart that I have written over the years for *The Nugget*.

# The human-dog bond

Jill lost her husband a few years ago to cancer, and during the months following his passing, deep loneliness set in. After all, they had been together for over 30 years. One of her friends advised her to get a dog because they make great companions, so she did. A year later Jill and her furry best friend traveled everywhere together, a special bond had been formed.

Pet parents talk about their dogs like they're part of the family, and it often seems as though their furry companion is another one of the kids.

In fact, when you speak to folks about what it's like to live with a dog, many will tell you that they discovered a degree of solace that's extremely difficult to achieve in relationships with people. That it's a way of experiencing solitude without the loneliness.

And now behavioral science is starting to reveal how this friendship/bond came to be.

Less than 20 years ago, scientific teams led by psychologist Michael Tomasello of the Max Planck Institute for Evolutionary Anthropology in Germany and Vilmos Csanyi in Budapest, independently published research papers on how family dogs can follow human pointing gestures to find hidden food. Maybe that doesn't sound like much, but that work marked the birth of a thriving field of investigation into the biological foundations of the human-dog bond.

Since then researchers have learned that most people and their pooch live in an attachment relationship, just like mothers and infants. Not only do they enjoy one another's company, but humans help dogs navigate modern society, and dogs, in return, help humans when they lack a specific ability, such as sight.

Dogs are unique in the animal kingdom because they have figured out how to join the community of an entirely different species, which is evidence of sophisticated social competence. In other words, dogs have a good set of social skills, including the abilities to form attachments, regulate aggression, learn and follow rules, provide assistance and participate in various group activities.

It's a win-win situation for both species - but maybe humans get the better end of the deal.

Dogs can learn by watching us, which helps them master the rules in fitting into human groups. Dogs are often admired for their emotional sensitivity.

For years academic researchers refused to attribute emotions to animals. That attitude is changing slowly.

Another reason for the strong bond between dogs and humans is a chemical connection that happens in a loving gaze.

Takefumi Kikusui, a professor of veterinary medicine at the Companion Animal Research Lab at Azabu University in Japan, wondered exactly what dogs are getting out of their affectionate gazing at humans. In the a new study in the journal Science, Kikusui and his colleagues measured the oxytocin levels of dogs and their pet parents before and after the pairs spent 30 minutes together. And after they spent quality time petting, playing, and gazing into their furry friend's eyes, both the people and dogs showed increases in the levels of oxytocin.

Oxytocin, often called the "love hormone," performs various actions in humans, such as reducing stress, and it also triggers the onset of labor. But in mammals, one of its key roles is to help a parent and infant bond. In humans, both moms and babies get a spike in oxytocin during breast feeding, and they will spend hours gazing at each other, which is nature's way of forming a bond.

The findings may help explain one of the most puzzling stories in human history: how a predatory, fearsome wolf transformed into man's best friend. Kikusui speculated that, at some point early in the domestication of dogs, a small group of naturally more friendly dogs may have gazed at humans for bonding.

More than one third of all Americans live with dogs today. Americans are in the midst of a genuine love affair with dogs: people are spending more money on their furry friends than ever before, and they are indulging their companions with more services than ever before, such as doggie daycare, doggie summer camp, doggie clothes and high-end doghouses.

So this dance is about love. It's about attachment that's mutual and it's about a kind of connection that's virtually unknowable in human relationships because it's essentially wordless.

# Adopting a dog when you have kids

Your 7-year-old son and your 1-year-old pooch are playing in the room next to you, when suddenly you hear a growl coming from your dog. You race into the room and find your son trying to get the family dog to sit in a chair. Your son explains they were just playing a game and Rover needed to be sitting in that chair.

Luckily you were nearby, but things could have gotten out of hand; your child could have been bitten.

Young children are not able to interpret a dog's language, and the dog is incapable of communicating in other ways. Almost all dog bites are a result of failure on the parents' part to recognize and prevent potential problem situations.

Although dogs are capable of learning to control their behavior and not bite, and older children can learn to leave the dog alone, adult supervision is essential. Small children should never be left alone with any dog, no matter how reliable he has been before. Small children don't recognize a warning, such as a growl, when they hear one and very young children (under the age of 6) don't know what a growl means. A responsible adult needs to be on the scene to prevent any aggressive behavior by the dog and to keep her child from putting himself in danger.

Not every dog is right for a child and not every child is right for a dog. Your child will need to be trained on how to treat a dog, and Rover will need to be trained for tolerance, besides strict obedience training when around your child.

So, plan on spending lots of time training your dog and your child when bringing a new dog into your home with young family members.

Obedience training and socialization are absolute musts for a dog that will be spending time with children. Remember that a dog will act according to his instincts if he doesn't receive proper training or if that training isn't kept up through regular practice. Your dog needs to be taught to obey commands under all conditions no matter how distracting. Just like when your dog responds to "come" could save his life one day, an immediate response to the command "leave it" could save a child from serious injury.

The best approach to adopting a dog when you have children is to wait until your child is over 5. Researchers have found that children 7 or older can be ready to start developing a rewarding relationship with a new furry friend.

Take your time when looking for a dog, educate yourself about dog breeds. Finding the right dog for your child requires some detective work. Certain breeds can play a genetic role in a pet's personality and there are certain breeds that are more suitable for kids.

All ages of dogs have their advantages and disadvantages to consider. Puppies require more time and care and will need training not to play bite, and jump up on your kids. And a puppy's baby teeth are razor sharp until around four months of age when they get their adult teeth. An older dog may have pain and medical issues that limit their patience, especially around children. So the best choice for most families is a young adult dog that has previously lived successfully with children. You need to look for a pooch that obviously loves kids and doesn't merely tolerate them.

According to the Association of Professional Dog Trainers, families with very young children should look for a dog no smaller than 25-30 pounds, because a sturdier companion will not feel so vulnerable around children. And in general, very large dogs are often a better choice than very little dogs when the family includes babies and toddlers. Many of the large breeds such as Newfoundlands, hounds and retrievers, are generally more easy-going and are less likely to be hurt when accidentally stepped on or tripped over.

Dogs can help teach a child responsibility, patience, empathy and compassion. But remember, no young child is capable of properly training or completely caring for a new pooch, so the parent should always ultimately take full responsibility for the new dog.

Remember that a dog's basic temperament, instincts and training have the biggest effects on how that dog reacts to the world around him, and his levels of tolerance. A dog will react to situations according to what his instincts tell him unless these instincts are overridden by consistent training and socialization throughout his life. Remember to teach your children how to behave correctly and safely around all pets.

# Latchkey dogs

You've been working from home for two years and have a one year-old dog that you are able to give lots of quality time to. Then one day things change and you have to work outside the home.

A latchkey kid is a child who returns from school to an empty home because his or her parent or parents are away at work, or a child who must spend part of the day alone and unsupervised, as when the parents are away at work. There are now many afterschool programs that offer a safe place for the children of parents that have to work to survive.

But what about dogs who are home alone all day?

Pet parents across America struggle with their dog's emotions and their own when it comes to leaving their furry friend home alone while they go to work.

Today, because we consider dogs as family members, we're more sensitive to their need for stimulation and company.

Dogs are very social animals, and they would like nothing more than to be by your side 24/7. But that can't always be the case.

Some dogs suffer from separation anxiety when you leave them alone. Separation anxiety is triggered when dogs become upset because of separation from the human that they have become attached to.

According to the ASPCA, when treating a dog with separation anxiety, the goal is to resolve the dog's underlying anxiety by teaching him to enjoy, or at least tolerate, being left alone.

And Dr. Marty Becker, a veterinarian and coauthor of Chicken Soup for the Cat/Dog Lover's Soul, believes that if dogs must be left for a lengthy period, they should be given long, exerting walks before their pet parents depart, and left with chew toys or food puzzles so they have some stimulation while they're away.

You have a lot of options for when you need to leave your pooch alone. There are steps that can be taken to help make sure that your furry friend stays happy during the long day when you're gone.

Doggie daycare is one option, but not everyone can afford daycare, and not every dog is a good candidate. One thing to remember is that all dogs are different, and although canines should be socialized when they are puppies, not all dogs enjoy the social life, just like humans. You wouldn't bring a wallflower to a prom and you wouldn't leave a social butterfly at home with nothing to do.

Another common solution is to adopt a second dog to keep the first dog company. This can be a great idea - or create a bigger problem. There are many factors to consider, including the size, gender, energy, and temperament of your pooch and of a potential new dog. Talk to your veterinarian about whether a second dog is a good idea for your current dog. When the fit is right, adopting a second dog can bring a lot of happiness into everyone's life.

Another option is to hire a dog walker to provide exercise and maybe some playtime for your under-stimulated, home-alone pooch. Or you might know a friend or neighbor that has pets and wouldn't mind an extra dog along on his walk.

One of the best things you could do is to supply some good first-thing-in-the-morning exercise, because the best way to leave your dog is to leave him tired.

So try getting up a little early and provide the stimulation that your furry friend needs. Exercise helps calm your pooch down in more than one way. Physically, it tires him out, and it also can relieve anxiety because during a good workout your dog's brain releases endorphins, the feel-good chemical that reduces stress. Having an anxious and hyper dog at home alone is a recipe for disaster. So take your dog on a vigorous walk and maybe a game of fetch before you part ways.

You can also keep your pooch happy by providing him with the right kind of environment when you're not at home.

Animal behaviorists' agree that dogs need environmental stimulation, just as humans do.

A bored dog left to his own devices, whether inside or outside, may act out by chewing up your belongings or digging holes in the yard. Boredom can be as much of a cause for acting out as separation anxiety. For this reason, it's important to leave your furry friend with his favorite toys. Dog toys, like Kong, a nontoxic rubber toy with a hollow center, is a good option. When stuffed with food it provides dogs with a healthy outlet for their natural desire to chew. It will last longer when you freeze the food inside. Just hide a few food toys, like Kong, around the house or outside the house.

Remember, if your dog will spend his time outdoors when you're gone for a few hours, provide a warm enclosure in the cold months and shade during the warm months. The best-case scenario would be a doggie door, so he can go inside when he wants.

For some, the only way to avoid leaving their dog alone is to take him to work. Fortunately for pet parents, there's a growing national trend to allow dogs in the workplace. Many business owners in Sisters do just that.

If you currently don't have a dog, and you're considering adopting one; think about whether your lifestyle is appropriate to be sharing it with a furry friend. If you think your potential dog might be spending time home alone that should be a big aspect of your decision when choosing your new friend.

# Are dogs more intelligent than cats?

You and your closest friend rarely argue, except over one subject: Pet smarts. She knows a lot about cats and says they're smarter than dogs, but you as a pet parent with two dogs think she's wrong.

Who's right?

Scientists have recently designed certain techniques and measures that may give us the definitive answer. One of the measurements that animal psychologists and biologists have used to assess intelligence is called the Encephalization Quotient, and another is sociability.

In the late 1970s, psychologist Harry J. Jerison developed Encephalization Quotient or EQ. It's a mathematically sophisticated comparison of the actual brain weight of an animal compared to the expected brain mass for that animal's body size. Because this method accounts for the fact that larger animals usually have larger brains, it's a more accurate indicator of intelligence than simple brain size.

Social animals are typically brighter than solitary creatures. Because problem-solving is a regular part of social interaction, animals that live in groups have better opportunities for cognitive development. Social animals tend to have a higher EQ than those that live the solitary life.

Based on the EQ, the brightest animals on the planet are humans, followed by great apes, porpoises, and elephants. The dog is close behind elephants in its EQ.

Dogs have always been regarded as the more social animals while cats often go it alone.

By the standard of EQ, dogs come out slightly ahead of the intelligence game over cats. According to Wikipedia, there is only a 0.2 percent advantage to the dog. Such a minute difference may be the reason dog and cat parents argue about their favorite pets.

An Oxford University research team looked at how 500 species, both living and fossilized, have evolved over about 60 million years. The ones that lived in social groups had much larger brains, relative to body size, than those species that tend to be self-sufficient.

However, there is a real surprise that occurs in some recent data provided by two researchers at Oxford University. They wondered whether there had been evolutionary changes in the Encephalization Index over the years.

When we domesticate animals, especially a companion dog, we are placing new learning demands on it. Some of these demands are social in nature, such as understanding human communication, like words and gestures. So, dogs are really subjected to more pressure than cats. Therefore, over time it might be expected that dogs would show a greater rise in their EQ than cats.

It appears that, based on their EQ, dogs are becoming progressively more intelligent over time while cats have remained at much the same level of mental ability that they had when we first domesticated them.

But if pet parents would look at their cats from a different perspective and start giving them basic training like canines receive, felines just might catch up.

For right now, the age-old argument remains. A cat-lover will argue how their kitten is smarter than your puppy because he doesn't need any potty training. A dog lover will tell you that if cats were smarter, why aren't there any seeing-eye cats?

# The importance of socializing your dog

You recently adopted an adorable one year old dog from a shelter and found out that he has behavioral problems. You've worked hard to train your new furry friend by yourself, but now have to call in a professional trainer.

Rescuing a dog from an unknown background that could have been filled with neglect and abuse is filled with challenges. Often dogs surrendered to a shelter are in shock and are fearful. It could takes months of hard work just to get him comfortable around you and his new home, especially if he wasn't properly socialized to begin with.

A puppy that has been socialized at an early age can avoid behavior problems. This increases the likelihood that a dog will become a wonderful pet. A puppy, just like a child, can't grow into a healthy adult without your guidance and proper training.

Like humans, dogs are social creatures and your puppy needs interaction - with you, other people and other animals - beginning very early in life.

According to the ASPCA, a puppy is most accepting of new experiences between three and 12 weeks old. After that age, he will become much more cautious of anything he hasn't yet encountered. From about 12 to 18 weeks old the opportunity to easily socialize a puppy ends - and with each passing week it becomes harder to get the puppy to accept and enjoy something that he's initially wary of.

Your puppy needs to be exposed to people, animals, places, sounds and experiences that you expect him to be comfortable with in later life. Depending on the lifestyle you have planned for your furry friend, this might include the sight and sound of trains, garbage trucks, schoolyards of screaming children, crowds, cats or crying infants.

Proper socialization will help train your young dog to handle new experiences and challenges with acceptable, appropriate behavior.

An unsocialized dog is unlikely to cope well with changes in his environment or situation, making him difficult to handle for his pet parent, groomer, pet-sitter, and any people that come to visit.

What if you didn't have your furry friend as a puppy to properly socialize?

Regardless of the reason your dog wasn't socialized as a puppy, it doesn't mean he has to be kept confined to a life without dog friends or free play with others.

Here are a few tips on how to socialize your adult dog:

Dog walks (don't forget his leash) are great opportunities for your furry friend to see and possibly meet other dogs and people, as well as practice proper behavior when out and about. The goal should be to teach your adopted dog to behave calmly in public and on walks. Bring lots of tasty treats on your walks and reward Rover for sitting quietly and responding to his name while other dogs pass by at a safe distance.

Introducing dogs on a leash can be tricky, so keep introductions short. If he should bark at another dog, simply get his attention, using the treats, and walk him away from the situation. Once he calms down, continue your walk.

Don't rush things, but if you can introduce your dog to one new activity a week, it will go a long way toward helping them socialize and remain calm and well-behaved. Think of it this way; Rover will be acting as an observer at first.

For example, instead of just taking your unsocialized dog into a dog park and hoping for the best, you can expose them slowly by walking them around the outside of the fence and letting them see the dogs play and have fun. If your heart is set on social time with other dogs, start by introducing your furry friend to one dog at a time.

Invite a friend that has a gentle, easy-going dog to go on a walk with you and Rover. Allow polite distance between dogs while they get accustomed to each other. If both dogs appear relaxed throughout the walk, allow them to sniff each other briefly. Keep leashes loose and each interaction short. If either dog appears to be tensing up, call them apart using a pleasant voice.

If both dogs' bodies appear loose and tails are wagging, it's time to consider an off-leash session in one of your fenced yards with leashes dragging, using the same short sessions.

Teaching your adult dog appropriate behavior and protecting him from unwanted contact will go a long way in building a trusting relationship.

Give Rover space, time, and positive reinforcement when he behaves in a way that is pleasing to you.

# What is your dog's personality?

Is your dog really playful, or more laid-back? Does your furry friend easily get along with other dogs, or does he run away from new situations?

Your dog was born with a set of instinctive behaviors that he inherited from his parents. These behaviors can be grouped into three broad categories - prey, pack, and defense - called "drives." How many behaviors your dog has in each category, or drive, will determine his temperament, his personality and how he perceives the world.

But your dog's personality doesn't spring completely from genetics or inherited behaviors. Just like people, dogs are affected by their experiences and their environment - and their personalities can change over time.

Personality is the combination of characteristics or set of attributes such as sociability, aggressiveness, and willingness to please, that come together to form the social behavior of a species. Understanding who your dog is, based on his personality type, can help you figure out why he acts in a certain way and defines his behavior characteristics as an individual. Each dog has their own personality and just like people, dogs fall into different personality types.

We all know someone who's the life of the party, someone who is quiet and reserved, or someone who will do whatever it takes to get ahead.

Knowing your furry friend can help avoid potential behavior issues before they get out of control, when you understand how he may behave in certain situations.

The Confident Dog is a natural-born leader of the pack. He's dominant, self-assured, and can be provoked to bite. But he's a team player and responds best to a pet parent that is determined and decisive and has the potential to be a fine working or show dog. He can easily fit into a household provided his family knows what they are doing when it comes to training. This dog feels secure in his surroundings, and has a self-assuredness that shows in his body language.

The Independent Dog tends to be uninterested in people. This independent personality is perfectly happy being away from the crowd. Some breeds are independent by nature and capable of developing a very close bond with the family member who takes control as a fair, patient and strong leader. He may not be very affectionate and tends to have a low need for human companionship.

The Adaptable Dog is eager to please, and the easiest of the five personalities to train. Not as outgoing as the happy personality, this pooch gets along well with other dogs, cats, and people, including being reliable with kids. He's perfectly happy to follow commands from his pet parent. This is an easy-to-control dog - cooperative, gentle and affectionate, which makes him a great family pet. The adaptable personality would be a good candidate as a therapy dog.

The Laid-Back, Happy Dog is always ready to greet everyone he meets, whether he knows them or not. He gets along well with other dogs and cats. Pooches with a happy personality that haven't been taught basic commands, like sit or down, most likely will get into trouble for jumping up on people when they greet them. This dog can also become overly excited, especially around children. He will become well adjusted if he receives regular training and lots of exercise.

The Shy/Timid Dog needs a pet parent who can give calm, consistent, and patient understanding, with sensitivity to his needs and feelings. This pooch is insecure and extremely submissive. A timid dog doesn't like being in uncomfortable situations or around sudden or loud noises. He bonds very closely with his pet parent and requires regular companionship and encouragement to bring him out of his shell. Reward this dog with lots of praise for each little success because he needs that special reassurance from the one he bonds with to feel safe and secure.

Your furry family member may fit perfectly into one of these personality types or he may be a couple of types mixed together, but whatever personality type your dog is, enjoy your time with him and give him every opportunity to be the best he can.

Understanding your furry friend's personality helps you avoid unnecessary confrontations when training or socializing him. Not all dogs enjoy being around other canines, and there's nothing wrong with that. Knowing why your dog behaves the way he does is one part of building a strong bond that will last a lifetime.

## Do you and your dog get
## enough exercise together?

Wild dogs spend about 80 percent of their waking hours hunting and scavenging for food. Domestic dogs have been helping and working alongside us for thousands of years. Most dogs are bred for a specific purpose, such as hunting, farming, or protection.

Whether dogs were working for us or scavenging on their own, their survival once depended on lots of exercise and problem-solving.

But what about now?

Boredom and excess energy are two common reasons for behavior problems in dogs. They're meant to lead active lives, just like people.

Most dogs usually spend a little time outside, mainly when going out to "the bathroom." But many pet parents don't fully appreciate the added benefits from allowing their dogs to spend more significant time outdoors. Spending quality time with your dog, just 30 minutes together outdoors, will benefit both you and your furry friend.

Taking at least one outing per day will help keep you and your pooch physically fit, plus it gives him opportunities to explore the world. Walking your dog daily is a great place to start, but the real quality time comes when you're both interacting together. And there are many fun and exciting things you and your furry friend can do side by side.

Here are five easy backyard games to play with your dog:

"Fetch" is a standard backyard game for dogs with a decent retrieval instinct. Running to retrieve a ball or toy is great exercise, and reinforces the human-doggie bond.

It seems that some dogs don't need to be taught to retrieve a toy; it's almost a natural instinct. But for those who don't have that ingrained interest, try smearing peanut butter on it, and try using Rover's favorite toy or ball. Then you can reinforce the "picking up" behavior by first rewarding any contact with the ball with a treat. Of course there is always that one dog that is possessive and won't bring his toy back to you after retrieving it. Just show him you have treats once the ball is in his mouth, and then offer to trade the ball for a treat. Do this until your dog understands that if he chases and then releases the ball, something good happens. Hopefully, soon he will forget about the treats!

Agility is an athletic and competitive dog sport that requires a dog to navigate an obstacle course. You don't have to enroll your pooch in classes or compete to have fun, even in a small backyard. Inexpensive agility equipment is available online, or you can even make your own. Just choose the agility equipment that would best suit your type of dog such as jumps, tunnels, weave-poles, tire-jumps, chutes, or teeter-totters.

Another great game is "hide and seek" using treat-dispensing toys in the backyard. Once your dog understands how to use these toys, you can start hiding them in corners of the yard, or under bushes and behind trees to make the game even more challenging. You can even time Rover as he gets better and faster at finding the treats.

Digging in a sandbox is GREAT for dogs who like to dig. Use a child's sandbox with a cover so that neighborhood cats don't make it a litter box. Remember to use only clean sand that you can buy right at your local hardware store. Bury Rover's favorite chews or toys in the sandbox and give him a hint on how to dig them up. Soon he'll understand that he will be rewarded for his efforts, and you'll avoid having to fill in another hole along your fence.

And it's still warm enough for staying cool in the puppy pool. A shallow pool can mean hours of backyard fun during the summer months, when your dog may want to cool off with a dip. Toss apple slices, baby carrots, or your pooch's favorite treat in the pool for a kind of "bobbing for treats" game. This is also a great way to persuade skeptical dogs to get their feet wet.

There is still enough time for these or any other backyard games you can think of before the winter months, so take delight in the quality time that you and your furry family can spend together.

# Cancer in your pet

Finding out that your furry family member has cancer is very scary and confusing. Cancer is the leading cause of death in dogs, and it's all the more heartbreaking because we have little or no insight into the cause.

The National Canine Cancer Foundation estimates that one in three dogs will develop cancer. And according to the American Veterinary Medical Association, 50 percent of dogs over the age of 10 will die of cancer.

Cancer is a class of diseases in which cells grow uncontrollably, invade surrounding tissue and can spread to other areas of the body. As with people, dogs can get various kinds of cancer. The disease can be localized (confined to one area, like a tumor) or generalized (spread throughout the body).

Older dogs are much more likely to develop cancer than younger ones, and certain breeds are prone to specific kinds of cancers. Boxers, Boston terriers and golden retrievers are among the breeds that most commonly develop mast cell tumors.

Be proactive and watch out for any signs that your dog may have cancer, regardless of age. Here are 10 warning signs of cancer in your dog to watch out for according to the American Veterinary Medical Association:

- Lumps and bumps - abnormal swellings that persist or continue to grow.
- Sores that don't heal - or they heal, but keep recurring.
- Weight loss - especially sudden weight loss at a time when your dog is not on a diet.
- Loss of appetite - if your dog isn't really interested in food, something's wrong.
- Bleeding or discharge - from any body opening.
- Offensive odor - coming from your dog's mouth or other parts of the body.
- Difficulty eating or swallowing - your dog acts differently around the food and water bowls than usual.
- Lethargy - an obvious hesitation to exercise, or loss of stamina.
- Evidence of pain - persistent lameness or stiffness.
- Difficulty breathing, urinating, or defecating.

"In many cases, cancer in dogs is not a death sentence at all," said Deborah Knapp, DVM, professor of veterinary clinical sciences at Purdue University.

There are many forms of cancer that are curable.

If you find a lump anywhere on your furry friend, make an appointment for him with your veterinarian. The first step is typically a needle biopsy, which removes a very small amount of tissue for a sample. Radiographs, ultrasound, blood evaluation and other diagnostic tests may also be helpful in determining if cancer is present or if it has spread.

It may be something completely benign and Rover doesn't have cancer. But if he does, treatment options vary and depend on the type and stage of cancer. Common treatments include surgery, chemotherapy, radiation and immunotherapy.

Success of treatment depends on the form and extent of the cancer and the aggressiveness of the therapy.

Remember that early detection is best!

What could be better than curing your furry friend's cancer?

Avoiding the illness in the first place. No one has done any clinical trials or statistical studies that prove you can prevent cancer in at-risk dogs. But according to Stacey Hershman, DVM, a holistic veterinarian in Rockland County, New York, "Common sense and clinical experience make a strong case for avoiding anything that exposes an animal to known carcinogens or weakens the immune system."

Just like humans, dogs can live longer, healthier lives when they eat the right foods, get enough exercise, breathe clean air, drink clean water, and stay away from harmful substances.

# What does that yellow ribbon mean?

The sun is shining and you're out walking Rover. You know that as he's grown older he is more temperamental toward energized kids. A group of teenagers walking by notice how beautiful your pooch is and run over to pet him, and before you can stop them he growls and tries to bite. Luckily nobody gets hurt.

We may love man's best friend, but not all dogs are "people" dogs.

There's a new way to warn people if your four-legged family member is feeling grumpy or aggressive. It's called "The Yellow Dog Project." Yellow dogs are dogs that need space, but it is important to know that not all dogs wearing a yellow ribbon are aggressive. Dogs need space for a variety of reasons including recovering from surgery, when they're undergoing training, being rehabilitated, or just because they are nervous around people they don't know. Thanks to The Yellow Dog Project, these dogs now have a way to communicate this.

The idea is simple: If your dog doesn't like to be approached, tie a yellow ribbon around his collar or leash to signal that your pet needs some space. A yellow ribbon around a dog's collar or leash can also help children identify that they need to proceed with caution. The dog may not be child-friendly, may have fear or anxiety issues, or may be overly excited. Either way, it means caution should be applied when approaching.

The Yellow Dog Project is a nonprofit organization that is a global effort to help raise awareness and education around dogs that require a little extra distance.

Tara Palardy, from Alberta, Canada founded The Yellow Dog Project in 2012 to alert the public that not all dogs are social. She is a dog trainer and manager of a doggie daycare. Palardy got the idea for The Yellow Dog Project from a Swedish website, but she wanted to take her yellow ribbons worldwide. She created a logo, launched a website and started a Facebook page that attracted more than 20,000 followers. The Yellow Dog Project has already reached 45 countries and is regularly adding more followers through its Facebook campaign.

The Yellow Dog Project is very promising as it will not only protect animals, but their humans as well. If folks are aware of The Yellow Dog Project, it could save someone from being bitten or hurt.

Whoever is interested in learning more, and in spreading the word in their neighborhood right here in Sisters, you can go to www.theyellowdogproject. com. On The Yellow Dog Project's Facebook page you can find a large community of people passionate on this project, sharing stories of their dogs, and helping to take part in making The Yellow Dog Project go big. In addition, you can download flyers in various sizes at the website's home page.

Although a yellow ribbon is a great way to give your dog space and let others know not to approach, dog aggression can be difficult to deal with.

Overcoming aggression, no matter what the reason, can be achieved with patience and training. Enroll your yellow-ribbon dog in obedience classes. It is important to expose your pooch to other dogs in a controlled setting. An obedience class is an ideal environment to work on dog aggression. Rover will learn to socialize in a positive way with other dogs.

# The importance of grooming your dog

You've been busier than normal and haven't had time to groom or brush your long-haired Shetland sheepdog in quite a while. You've started to notice that he's been scratching a lot, even though he's already been treated for fleas and ticks. So you decide to bring him for a visit to the groomer, and what she discovers after bathing your furry friend is an underlying skin condition causing him to feel very uncomfortable and itchy.

Grooming isn't a canine luxury, it's a necessity - and you don't have to break the bank to keep Rover groomed. Grooming is essential to the health and comfort of your pet; it allows you as a responsible pet parent to spot health problems before they become serious, or even life-threatening. Grooming on a regular basis allows you to look and feel for lumps, bumps, and injuries.

Brushing helps to remove dirt and loose, dead hair and helps prevent mats and tangles.

Dirt and oils can accumulate under mats and cause painful skin infections. And that the mats themselves can be painful as they pull the skin underneath. Severe matting can even affect your furry friend's ability to see, walk, and eat normally.

If you find a mat in your pooch's hair, do not pull on it. Pulling can be painful. There are special brushes and combs available to help split the mat up.

With some dog breeds, grooming is a little more involved. Breeds such as collies, Alaskan malamutes, etc. are "double-coated" which means they have a downy undercoat underneath a harsher layer of long hair, and the down can mat like a layer of felt against the skin if left untended.

Each breed is different and some dogs - like a short-haired terrier - will be easy compared to a curly haired poodle. Some folks prefer to hire a professional groomer because they don't have the time to do it themselves.

Many dogs benefit from an occasional bath that goes along with brushing to remove dirt and excess skin oils that can sometimes cause skin conditions and unpleasant odors.

Another part of grooming that is important for your furry friend is nail-trimming. Keeping Rover's nails trimmed can help avoid some painful conditions such as torn or overgrown nails. Just like with brushing, trimming his nails gives you an opportunity to examine the area for problems like cracked pads, swelling or injuries.

Most dogs benefit from having their ears cleaned on a regular basis, but that takes practice for the pet parent, so talk to your veterinarian if you suspect any ear problems such as ear mites, cheat grass or possible infection.

Brushing your pet's teeth is also a part of grooming. Although many pet parents don't realize it, brushing your dog's teeth regularly can go a long way in preventing periodontal disease. According to the ASPCA, periodontal disease is being recognized as a widespread problem in pets.

Some dogs seem to naturally enjoy the feeling of being brushed. Others, however, find it uncomfortable. You can usually tell the dog that doesn't like being groomed, because when your furry friend sees the brush coming, his ears will go back and he may try to hide from you.

The easiest way to train your dog to endure the grooming process is to start when he is still a puppy, although that is not always possible because you may adopt an adult dog.

Grooming should be a relaxing time for both you and your dog. It can become a special time that you both share together.

If your furry friend doesn't like being brushed, you may need to help change the way he feels about grooming so that he can tolerate it better and even begin to enjoy it.

Start by going to a quiet area with him, a place where he enjoys being, such as outdoors on the porch. Bring a handful of extra tasty treats along with his brush. Try speaking softly to your dog; slowly and gently stroke him with the brush in a non-sensitive area.

# Dementia in dogs

After a lifetime of excited tail-wags, devoted companionship, and playing ball, it's no wonder your senior dog is beginning to show his age. Maybe his hearing has declined and his muzzle has grayed. Maybe his coat has begun to thin or maybe he is slow to rise and not as spry as his younger days.

Natural aging can change appearance, decrease mobility or dull the senses. If your older dog's personality has changed, he may be experiencing something much more serious than the usual signs of aging. If Rover seems confused, distant, or lost, he may be showing signs of Cognitive Dysfunction Syndrome (CDS).

More and more dogs are living into their senior years and, just like elderly humans, pets can suffer from a type of dementia.

With neurological signs similar to Alzheimer's disease in humans, CDS in dogs is caused by physical changes in the brain and its chemicals. And according to Donna Solomon, DVM at the Animal Medical Center of Chicago, it is a disease that involves the degeneration and loss of nerve cells within the brain of older pets resulting in behavioral changes.

Does Rover wake up in the middle of the night and pace back and forth? Or does he sometimes seem disoriented when trying to find the doggie door?

Due to the changes in your dog's brain you'll notice a deterioration of how your dog thinks, learns, and remembers, which may cause behavioral changes that can disturb the lives of both you and your furry family member.

According to the book *Decoding Your Dog,* by Steve Dale, the signs of CDS can be remembered is by the acronym DISHA.

Disorientation - Such as being confused or getting lost in familiar environments.

Interactions with humans and other pets have changed - such as changes in affection, or irritability.

Sleep-wake cycle changes such as increased sleep during the day or waking during the night.

House training and learned behaviors may deteriorate.

Activity levels alter and even include aimless wandering or even compulsive disorders such as excessive licking.

If you suspect that your furry friend has CDS, make an appointment with your veterinarian. Many people don't mention their dog's changes to their vets, believing it is just "old age," but a combination of a number of the above symptoms are not normal to the aging process and options are available to help treat or control CDS.

There are also many CDS symptoms shared with other serious medical conditions. For instance, decreased activity could be a sign of advanced arthritis, and if your dog isn't paying attention as he once did, it could be a result of hearing or vision loss, and incontinence could be from a serious urinary infection or kidney disease. So it is important to let your veterinarian eliminate other conditions before making a diagnosis of CDS.

Although there is no cure for CDS, there are multiple treatment methods to try to improve your dog's quality of life. Helping your furry friend cope with CDS and considering his needs when it comes to your home, its surroundings, and the environment, are the key.

Try to keep your dog awake during the day as much as possible so he can sleep easier at night. Try exercising Rover for 30 minutes a day. Try not to change or rearrange furniture. Increase mental stimulation, which might include food puzzles, interactive toys, extra grooming, doing tricks and encourage learning new ones.

Eliminate clutter to create wide pathways throughout the house. Encourage gentle and involved short play sessions.

And please remember to have a daily routine for feeding and walking. Dogs thrive on routine.

Keep your patience and compassion. Your furry family member's world has changed, but every effort should be made to show him that your love, respect, and pride of his past and present abilities have not changed and never will.

# Give your dog a job

Rover stays home five hours a day while you're working. He naps most of the day on his usual spot that is now worn down on the couch. He's bored because he has nothing to keep him mentally and physically stimulated.

Dogs are amazing creatures and they are our wonderful loving and nonjudgmental friends, but they also have an innate and instinctual need to work.

Dogs need a job that provides appropriate release for their mental and physical energies. Even before domestication, dogs had a job; they worked to survive. Pack members worked to define, protect, and retain their territory.

Domestic dogs have been helping and working alongside us for thousands of years, and most are bred for a specific purpose. Many of our four-legged friends have regular jobs, and all of us depend on these working dogs to do those jobs well.

There are service dogs, police dogs, search-and-rescue dogs, therapy dogs and herding dogs. They pull sleds, herd farm animals, hunt for game, search for missing persons and inspect luggage for illegal drugs. Their job possibilities are endless.

There are hundreds of breeds of dogs, and they come in all shapes and sizes. Many breeds have been trained for specific jobs that fit their type, for instance among the dog breeds that perform police work are German shepherds.

What if you don't have a dog that is appropriate for search and rescue? What if there isn't a flock of sheep at your disposal for your border collie? It isn't necessary to quit your job to take up duck-hunting to keep your dog busy working.

Nowadays pet parents lead busy lives, and their pooches often end up spending a portion of their day home alone. Give your dog "jobs" to do when he's by himself. Dogs are mentally, physically, and emotionally healthier and happier when they fulfill a "sense of purpose." Even your couch potato will benefit from having defined "jobs" in your home.

Start with food puzzle toys when you're away. They are sturdy food containers usually made of hard rubber or plastic, that holds food or treats inside but don't give your dog easy access to the food. They have holes on each end or on the sides, so your four-legged friend must work by pawing, rolling or licking the toy to get the food to come out. Food puzzles require time, patience and problem-solving, which is great mental stimulation for Rover. If you want to make it even more fun, try hiding a couple of food puzzle toys around the house.

You've finally returned home from work and your furry friend hears you unlock the door and is anxious to greet you. Maybe Rover can find a good task during your usual walk with him.

Don't underestimate the value of a good walk or jog with your dog; it gives him a job opportunity by sniffing out different scents, especially if you try a new route every now and then.

Start looking for ideal places for you and your dog to play. A fun game or "task" for your dog is learning to play Frisbee. Many dogs love to play Frisbee, although most dogs don't know how to catch a flying disc. With a little patience you and Rover can learn to do this fun and rewarding activity. Take it a step further and enter your dog into a flying disc competition with other dogs.

Train your dog on an agility course. There are agility courses set up in specific areas, like off-leash dog parks. Or make your own course in the backyard. Agility is a sport that has swept the dog world in recent years. Many agility competitions are open to any dog, regardless of a pedigree. The sport teaches shy dogs confidence and gives lively dogs a positive channel for their energy.

If you cannot determine what it would be that your dog would excel in, you can begin with basic obedience with a good trainer who is knowledgeable in each dog group and can evaluate your dog individually for his capabilities.

There are endless jobs that you can train your four-legged friend to do, including everyday little tasks like fetching the paper or putting his own toys away.

For centuries, humans have been privileged to have the benefit of dogs as loving and faithful companions. Dogs have accomplished amazing feats to earn the title "Man's Best Friend." Dogs can perform tasks that demand great responsibility. Dogs have saved many lives while working in the field of emergency response, and have aided soldiers in wartime. They serve as companions to the disabled and serve as eyes and ears to the blind and deaf.

Life is better with the help of these dedicated canines.

# Longevity and your pet

Max the terrier lived a very long life. He recently passed away in May 2013 at the age of 29 years, 282 days. He was heralded as the oldest living dog, according to Wikipedia. The oldest living cat, Poppy at age 24, passed away this year. She reigned as the oldest living cat according to the Guinness Book of World Records.

Dogs like Max and cats like Poppy are outside the norm, but they may be an indicator of an increasingly longer pet lifespan. Veterinarians say it's not unusual for some dogs and cats to reach 15 years or more, and they're seeing more and more pets do so.

Just as the average life expectancy for people keeps reaching closer to the century mark, you will continue to see the same parallels in the pet population. Just like in people, genetics is a part of the equation, so to a significant degree how long an individual dog or cat is likely to live is pre-programmed.

The choices you make for your pet can go a long way in affecting their lifespan. Pet gerontology expert and veterinarian Richard T. Goldston, in St. Petersburg, Florida, says the improvement is a combination of more responsible pet parents, a stronger human-animal bond, and better veterinary care and pet nutrition.

Most dogs, depending on size, can live 10 to 15 years if they are in good shape mentally and physically, and most (indoor) cats generally live from 12 to 18 years of age.

Here are some tips that you as a pet parent can do to extend and improve the quality of your furry friend's life:

Neutering or spaying a pet may help extend their lifespan because the surgery drastically lowers the risk of certain kinds of serious health concerns including complications from pregnancy and delivery such as dystocia, and certain cancers that affect the mammary glands and reproductive organs.

Maintaining your pet's teeth is very important because tooth decay is a very common and dangerous health problem. Tooth decay not only creates dental problems; it can cause infections throughout the body, especially in the heart and kidneys. Most dogs and cats are not going to have picture-perfect teeth or fresh breath like a human, but their teeth should be reasonably clean. Start brushing your furry friend's teeth when he is young, if you can. You can buy toothpaste and toothbrush kits for dogs and cats.

Unfortunately, the obesity crisis has affected animals as well as people. Rover or Kitty can become overweight if they eat a lot of fatty human foods or even if they are eating too much pet food and don't get enough exercise. You can extend your four-legged friend's life if you make an effort to keep him at a healthy weight at all times.

Folks nowadays see the benefit of exercising more; it can extend your life, the same goes for Kitty or Rover. Ideally your pet should get at least an hour of exercise every day to improve their health and regulate their weight. Yes, you can exercise your cat either on a harness or just having playtime.

As the saying goes, an ounce of prevention is worth a pound of cure, and regular checkups with your veterinarian can help detect diseases and health problems early on, while they can still be treated. Vaccinations can save lives. Experts recommend that dogs and cats should visit the vet at least once a year when they are fully grown, and two to four times a year while they are puppies.

Just like humans, stress can have a negative effect on your furry friend. There should be some type of routine where your pet can get exercise and have time to be part of the family but also have time for rest. It takes a lot of energy to run around with the family and keep up with all the excitement, so they need time to sleep on their own, too.

As you can see, the key to longevity in your pet's life is to provide them with a healthy lifestyle, which includes maintaining a healthy weight, daily exercise, relaxation, and regular checkups.

Just think of your furry friend's well being in the same way that you would think of a human family member.

# Keep your dog safe in snowy weather

The biggest snowstorm in years just transformed your yard into a winter wonderland, and your furry friend can't wait to get out there and play in the white stuff.

Most dogs can't resist rolling in fresh snow or running through tunnels you're shoveling to get to the street. Refereeing a good snow ball fight is fun for Rover, too.

Just like a kid, your pooch might not know when it's time to come in from the cold, so it's up to you as a good pet parent to bring him in before problems occur.

Walking your pooch in snow and ice can be hard on paws, particularly on pads that are not toughened up, or for a dog that is a breed which doesn't tolerate cold well. The three main problems that can affect your furry friend's paws in cold snowy weather are overly cold paws, buildup of ice balls and de-icing (salt) products. All these can cause a dog pain, and potentially damage to one or more paws.

Most dogs do not seem to have a problem with snow if the temperature is at or just below freezing. Each dog is different, and some tend to have a problem with overly cold paws during extremely cold and snowy days.

De-icer can be irritating to dogs' paws, and toxic if Rover licks an excessive amount from his paws (it can cause gastrointestinal upset and vomiting). Always use pet-safe de-icer, but it's still best that your pet not ingest it.

For many dogs, the main problem with snow is the buildup of ice balls under the pads and in between the toes. Ice balls can be as irritating to a dog's foot as a pebble in a shoe can be for a human. Since the ice balls are formed around the hair on the paw pads, they need to be broken up as gently as possible without pulling them out.

Remember to check Rover's paws after coming in from a snowy walk, particularly when you've walked in areas that could have been treated with de-icer. Be sure to check between the toes and look at his pads for any cracks or sore spots. Gently wash off your dogs' paws with a warm cloth upon returning home.

Did you know that the dogs (mushers) in the Iditarod Sled Race wear booties to protect their paws from abrasions? Dog boots aren't for all dogs, but they can help with many of the problems that some pooches have with snow. They keep their feet warmer, prevent the buildup of ice balls and they stop de-icing products from getting on the pads and between the toes.

More than irritated paws can affect your furry friend during snowy days.

If you have a medium-to-long-haired pooch, watch out for the abominable snowdog after a romp or two in the white stuff. Ice balls stuck in Rover's fur can be a big mess. Be gentle when you remove these frozen ice balls. Use a warm, moist towel to help melt the balls and then use a dry towel to dry your dog's coat. Do not try to pull them out of Rover's fur; it can be painful.

You and your dog enjoy playing in the snow, but you also need to keep safety in mind.

Don't leave your dog outside in the cold for long periods of time. Extreme cold poses a frostbite threat to your dog's nose and ears.

Remember to provide plenty of fresh water. Your pooch is just as likely to get dehydrated in the winter as in the summer. Snow is not a satisfactory substitute for water.

Our dogs cannot talk to us when they are sick or in pain. As a responsible pet parent, it is important to pay special attention to your dog's well being during the winter season.

# Common dog myths debunked

Call them legends or even old wives' tales, but don't call them facts. Whether it's a tip from a neighbor or something you remember from long ago, myths about dogs can steer you in the wrong direction.

These myths have been around since the domestication of dogs, and some of them stick around even today. Here are some misconceptions about dogs that just won't die:

It was once believed that dogs could see only in black and white. Many people still think this is the case. Dogs do see in color, but they see differently than most people do and are less able to distinguish between colors. Veterinary ophthalmologists have determined that dogs see like humans who have red/green color blindness. Dogs' eyes have receptors for blue and green shades, but not for red shades. As a result, it appears that dogs cannot easily distinguish between yellow, green and red, but they can identify different shades of blue, purple and gray.

"Can't teach an old dog new tricks" is a myth that has become a popular cliché over the years, (usually referring to people). The fact is old dogs not only learn new tricks, but they thrive when being trained. While it isn't as easy to teach an older dog new tricks, it can still be accomplished. A senior dog might no longer possess the reflexes or energy of an enthusiastic puppy, but with some patience on the pet parent's part, introducing new skills to an old dog is perfectly achievable.

Another old wives tale, which is probably the biggest dog-health misconception around, is that if your dog's nose is warm or dry, it indicates he's sick. The moisture content or even the temperature of a dog's nose is not measurements of his health.

For instance, your pooch's nose is often dry and/or warm if he has just woken up, and this is perfectly normal. But if his nose is persistently dry and crusted, it could be a sign of a health problem; just check with your vet.

Have you ever seen your dog eat grass? The myth is that a dog will eat grass to induce vomiting, and it's true that dogs will often throw up after eating a lot of grass. However, this does not mean they ate that grass to induce vomiting, or that it is somehow a sign of illness.

While nobody knows the exact reasons why dogs eat grass, it is possible that they just actually like grass. Some dogs like to graze, while others chomp.

Enough grass in the stomach can create minor irritation and cause Rover to vomit. Some experts believe that a dog's taste for grass goes back to the days when dogs' ancestors, such as wolves, ate the stomach contents of its prey, usually grass, leaves, etc. Regardless of the reason, it's relatively harmless as long as the grass is not chemically treated.

So you think that a few table-scraps are okay for your dog? Think again. One ounce of cheddar cheese for a 20-pound dog is like a human eating more than one-and-a-half chocolate bars. In other words, table scraps are empty calories for dogs. Your precious pooch needs precisely balanced nutrition for his specific life stage to continue to remain healthy.

For instance, eating scraps of ham could create gastrointestinal problems and pancreatic concerns. Do your furry friend a favor and stick to his nutritional dog food and treats.

Most people think that if a dog's tail is wagging that is a sign of a happy dog. But that is not always the case. And this happens to be a dangerous misconception that sometimes leads to dog bites. While tail-wagging often means that a dog is happy or excited, it can also suggest anxiety or even fear, which can be aggression triggers.

Some people believe that just letting their dog out in the yard is enough exercise, and that, too, is myth. Dogs need mental stimulation as well as physical activity. If you leave your dog out in the yard alone, they might not get much of either. It's important to take them for walks, play fetch or simply run around together. Of course different-sized dogs may require different levels of activity, and not only will it make for a happier, healthier dog but it will also help strengthen your relationship.

# Deafness in dogs

Lately you've noticed that your well-trained furry friend hasn't been coming when called and seems distracted. Could it be hearing loss?

Some dogs can have a temporary hearing loss due to wax build-up in their ear canals, especially dogs with a lot of hair around their ears. A total loss of hearing can be due to a host of causes such as severe, untreated ear infections, old age or injuries. One or both ears may be affected.

Some dogs are born deaf, which is known as congenital deafness, and it is more common with specific breeds such as Dalmatians and boxers. White dogs also tend to have a high occurrence of deafness. Although researchers still aren't sure what causes congenital deafness, they do know it's most common in dogs with white or nearly white heads.

Dogs that have hearing loss may appear disobedient and ignorant of commands. A dog with extreme hearing loss will not typically respond if you snap your fingers next to its ears or if you make an unfamiliar noise that would normally cause a reaction from him.

Please take your pooch to the veterinarian if you suspect any hearing loss. Your vet can initially examine your dog's ear canal for wax accumulation, infections, inflammation, injury or a foreign object. You might be surprised that a wax build-up could have been the problem and that it is relieved once the plug of wax was removed.

You may have recently purchased a white puppy and after a couple of weeks found out that your new furry friend may have been born deaf. If you suspect your pup might be deaf, try this test: wait until he is asleep or not looking at you and make a loud noise behind him. Make sure he can't see your movement, or feel any vibrations, like you stomping on the floor. If your dog ignores you and appears to be deaf you might want to ask for a test called the Brainstem Auditory Evoked Response procedure, or BAER. During this test, electrodes are placed under the dog's scalp to read the brain's response to a series of clicks directed into each ear.

Training a deaf dog isn't difficult. There are many deaf dog rescue organizations that encourage people to adopt a deaf dog. These special-needs dogs can make wonderful pets. You simply communicate with your pooch using signs and body language instead of words.

According to Dick Russell, a dog trainer near Baton Rouge, Louisiana, who has worked with more than 100 deaf dogs in the past 20 years, "It's as easy to train a deaf dog as a hearing dog. The only difference is you use hand signals instead of verbal commands." The secret according to Russell is having a clear hand signal for each action you want your dog to learn, and always being consistent. Deaf dogs, just like hearing dogs, require time, patience and energy devoted to training and socialization to help them become well-adjusted and well-mannered. As with any pooch, it's important to have a trusting relationship and build your dog's confidence through positive interactions.

If you have an older dog that is in the beginning stages of hearing loss, start to incorporate non-verbal cues into training. Reward your furry friend when he comes to you by cue of the hand gesture. Gradually wean him off the verbal command until he is able to follow only hand signals.

One of the most important commands you can teach your deaf dog is the "watch me" command. It is one of the first commands your deaf dog should learn when you start training with hand signals. Your dog will constantly check in by always looking directly at you.

Of course, there are some common-sense steps pet parents of a deaf dog should take.

The first is keeping your furry friend on a leash or in a fenced yard for his safety. A deaf dog can't hear a car or other danger coming.

To better keep track of your pooch, try putting a bell on his collar and make sure that on Rover's tag it says "DEAF" along with your contact information.

Always let your dog know of your presence around the house. A dog that is deaf will not be able to hear you approaching and may be frightened if you suddenly appear. One way is to lightly pet your pooch on the back and give him a treat when he turns toward you.

Rewarding your dog with treats and physical affection is a must, since a deaf dog cannot hear verbal praise.

Deaf dogs can live normal lives; they just require a little extra care and attention. Deaf dogs can do agility, obedience, and can be wonderful therapy dogs.

# The importance of dental health

You just got back from a yearly routine exam for Rover, and your vet told you that it's time to start brushing your 3-year-old collie's teeth. To top it off he gave you a soft doggie toothbrush with special toothpaste just for dogs. He showed you the simple steps of how to brush your furry friend's teeth, and explained to you how proper maintenance of Rover's teeth could be a lifesaver in the long run.

According to the American Veterinary Association, oral disease is the number-one health problem in dogs and cats, with 85 percent of dogs 5 years or older having periodontal disease. And it's alarming when you realize that unhealthy teeth spread infection and disease to other parts of the body like the heart, and can cut a pet's life-span by five years.

Periodontal disease develops when food particles and bacteria collect along the gum line and form soft deposits called plaque. Whenever your pooch eats, bits of food and bacteria collect around the gum line and form plaque. Over time, the plaque turns into rock-hard tartar. Tartar irritates the gums and results in inflammation, called gingivitis. Your dog's gums will turn from a healthy pink color to red, and you may notice some bad breath. If the tartar isn't removed it will accumulate under your dog's gums, eventually pulling the gums away from the teeth and creating small open spaces, or pockets, which are collection points for even more bacteria. If the problem progresses to this point, your pooch has developed irreversible periodontal disease. At this point, your dog can experience severe pain, lose teeth, form abscesses in his mouth and could develop a bacterial infection that can spread through the bloodstream to the kidneys, liver, heart or brain.

How quickly plaque, tartar and gum disease develop in your dog's mouth depends on a number of factors including his age, overall health, diet, breed, genetics, and the care his teeth receive from both you and your veterinarian.

Since periodontal disease is irreversible, now is a great time to get started on a regular oral-care regimen for your pooch.

So brushing your furry friend's teeth isn't just about fresh breath. It's an essential part of good oral care, and good oral care is important to your dog's overall health. If you start brushing your pet's teeth as a puppy you can prevent them from getting periodontal disease as an adult and that will save you costly dental bills.

Gum disease in dogs has been linked to canine heart disease. A study, conducted by Dr. Larry Glickman at Purdue, examined the records of nearly 60,000 dogs with some stage of periodontal disease and about 60,000 without, and revealed a correlation between gum and heart maladies.

According to Glickman, their data showed a clear statistical link between gum disease and heart disease in dogs. The correlation was even stronger when it came to endocarditis, or inflammation of the heart valves. In the dogs with no periodontal disease, about 0.01 percent were diagnosed with endocarditis, compared to 0.15 percent of the Stage 3 periodontal disease dogs.

While studies clearly show a significant link between periodontal disease and heart disease in both humans and dogs, exactly how one leads to the other isn't yet well-understood. Researchers suspect, however, that the culprit is bacteria in the mouth which enters the bloodstream. Mouth tissue, known as oral mucosa, is rich with blood vessels which hasten the speed at which bacteria can enter your dog's bloodstream and travel throughout his body.

If your dog has periodontal disease, the surface of his gums is weakened and compromised. The breakdown of gum tissue is the door through which mouth bacteria enters her bloodstream. And if your furry friend's immune system doesn't kill off the bacteria circulating in her blood, it can reach his heart and infect it.

It's ideal to brush your dog's teeth daily, just like you brush your own. However, if your schedule doesn't allow that, aim to brush his teeth at least several times a week.

Of course the best time to start is when he is a puppy, it's easier for him to get used to having his teeth brushed, but grown dogs can learn to become comfortable with getting their teeth cleaned also.

You can get a doggie toothbrush and toothpaste at any good pet-supply store. Do NOT use regular human toothpaste for your pooch. Most human toothpastes include fluoride, which is extremely poisonous to dogs. And since dogs don't rinse, even without fluoride the paste is not meant to be digested.

With some dogs it may not be so easy, and if the tooth brushing ends in blood, sweat, or tears, there are still choices you can make to help improve your dog's oral health. Crunchy kibble is better for our furry friend's teeth than soft food, as soft food is more likely to stick to the teeth and cause decay. There are many synthetic bones and chew toys that are specially designed to strengthen your dog's gums and teeth. Giving your dog a good specially made bone to chew on can help rid buildup and keep teeth strong.

Even with healthy teeth, just like you, your dog should have his teeth checked by your vet every six to 12 months.

Dental care can be a pain in the neck for humans and dogs, but proper maintenance can be a money-saver in the long run, and even a lifesaver. Letting it go can lead to costly and often painful vet visits down the road. Keep your dog's mouth clean, and you'll both be smiling!

# Should your dog be leashed?

It's a sunny spring day and you and your leashed mini-poodle are taking a leisurely stroll in the park. You're smiling and his tail is wagging. Suddenly, out of nowhere, a Great Dane bounds by to say hello, he's unleashed and his human is running over to catch him. Meanwhile your pooch is shaking from fright. The relaxing walk that you two were taking is over.

Does Oregon have a leash law? No. However, it does have an "at large" ordinance. According to Deschutes County animal control, County Code 6.08.15 defines "at large" to mean a dog or other animal found off the premise of the owner or keeper while the dog or animal is not under the complete control of a capable person. This would allow for dogs that are trained to be off the leash; however it would require them to be under the control of the handler.

But, as a responsible pet-owner, should you allow your dog to run free, or be off-leash while you walk together? What could happen while your pooch is off leash, even with you nearby?

Dogs get distracted. Even if your pooch is under strong verbal command, it's all too easy for him to have "selective hearing" when running around off-leash. You may think you have Rover under control, but if a cat went running under his nose he just might chase it. What if something suddenly spooked your dog, like a vehicle backfiring? He could end up out in the street and in that moment get hit by a car.

You may own a friendly dog, but what about all the other dogs? Your dog could be attacked by another dog if that animal considers your dog to be invading his territory. Or another dog may see your unleashed pet as a potential danger to his human. Your dog could be seriously hurt.

While off-leash, your dog could accidently scare an elderly person and cause him to fall. Remember, you are responsible for your dog's behavior.

Your dog could end up eating something unhealthy. Dogs love to put things in their mouth, and you may not notice him chewing on a poisonous plant.

A dog that is not on a leash could defecate in an area that you may not notice. This could be extremely annoying to the other people in the area.

Our furry friends do seem to be happier off-leash; it's their nature to be able to roam, smell, roll, splash through streams and chase squirrels up trees.

There are off-leash dog-parks where your pooch can frolic and play, which includes socializing with other dogs.

Many people bring their dogs along to the numerous hiking trails in Central Oregon. It's wonderful exercise for Rover.

For some hikers, the rewards of hiking with their dog off-leash far outweigh the drawbacks.

Rachel Baum, a dog-behavior therapist and master trainer, recommends that anyone about to head into the forest trails, know their dog well before taking him along.

Bring a leash with you in case you need it. This could include for encounters with wildlife - cougars or bears - or conditions like mud that you would like to avoid.

Beyond safety issues, unleashed dogs, even when friendly, can still be a pest to other hikers, particularly when they beg for food or are wet and dirty. So if you're bringing Rover along on your next outing and want to hike with him off-leash, be prepared to rein in his enthusiasm and keep him under control. Not everyone loves your dog as much as you do.

Wherever you decide to take your dog for an outing, whether it's a park, walking down the street or hiking on a trail, remember to be courteous of others.

# Poisonous plants and dogs

The combination of a voracious appetite and natural curiosity can lead to trouble for dogs. Plants that are poisonous to dogs can be found in your home, your yard and in the wild, and sometimes all it takes is a little bite to lead to an emergency trip to the veterinarian.

Many types of plants and flowers are toxic to dogs. Effects range from mild to severe, depending on the type of plant and the quantity consumed. Some plants will only cause slight stomach upset, while others can cause seizures, coma, or even death.

Toxic plants that are already on your property should be removed, or, if you are planning to get new plants or flowers, educate yourself with a list (www. petmd.com) for all poisonous plants that can affect your furry friend. Do not keep toxic plants inside your home.

_Jodi Schneider McNamee_

Among the first blooms that signify the arrival of spring, daffodils and tulips are a cheerful addition to the garden, but they contain poisonous alkaloids that can cause vomiting, diarrhea and convulsions. The bulbs are the most dangerous part of the plant.

Azaleas and rhododendrons are a beautiful addition to the greenery and color of a landscape. However the bark, leaves and foliage all contain toxins deadly to dogs.

The toxicity of grapes to dogs was once thought to be an urban legend. The truth is that even a small serving can cause vomiting and diarrhea, while larger amounts can lead to kidney failure. Researchers aren't yet sure what exactly causes this reaction. Until the cause of the toxicities is better identified, the safest course of action is to avoid feeding grapes to your dog.

With its broad variegated leaves, the dieffenbachia (Dumb Cane) is often recommended as an ideal houseplant for natural air purification. But if you choose to have one in your home, be sure it's well out of Fido's reach. When eaten, it not only burns the mouth and throat but causes the esophagus to swell, potentially blocking his airway.

Onions are always a spring favorite and grow easily in our cold climate. Onions pose a significant risk of developing hemolytic anemia, a condition where a dog's red blood cells die. If the anemia is not treated, it can be fatal.

Mushrooms pop up everywhere - in yards, in the woods, in parks, alongside roads, and in salad bars. Some dogs, like people, like to eat them. They can be a gourmet delicacy or deadly poison.

Mushroom hunting is booming in the Pacific Northwest, a region long regarded as a mushroomer's paradise. Dogs, like people, often like mushrooms and are attracted to them by scent and sight and will ingest them willingly.

Unfortunately, they can make your furry friend ill, and in some cases can be fatal to them. Dogs just don't seem capable of discerning the difference

58

between the edible and the toxic. To be on the safe side, it's best not to allow Rover to eat any wild mushrooms at all.

Mushroom poisoning in dogs, is an underestimated problem in North America. Because of the amount of time dogs spend outdoors or in wooded areas, they can be particularly prone to mushroom poisoning. Pet parents need to be vigilant about looking for mushrooms when walking their dogs in parks, along the roadside and on trails.

Poisonous mushrooms can cause a number of symptoms within six hours of being ingested. Watch for vomiting, diarrhea, excessive salivation, lethargy and seizures.

This is a wonderful time of year for both you and your furry friend to be hiking outdoors or in the yard. Be careful and observant for your pet's sake so that you do not have to take an emergency trip to your veterinarian.

If your pet gets into any suspected toxins or uncertain plants, it is best to contact animal poison control at 888-426-4435, www.ASAP.org or call your veterinarian immediately. It could save their life.

# Pets, parasites, and people

You love spring; it's a time for renewal and the little green buds on the trees outside are beginning to blossom, your daffodils have bloomed and the air is warm. But you noticed that Rover doesn't seem so happy lately. He's started to scratch a lot.

April is Parasite Awareness Month: It's important to keep your four-legged friends free of parasites.

What is a parasite? A parasite is a plant or animal that lives on or inside another living organism (called a host). A parasite is dependent on its host and lives at the host's expense.

There are internal parasites such as heartworms, hookworms, tapeworms and roundworms that live inside the body of a host. And there are external parasites such as fleas, ticks, and ear mites that live on the outside of the body of their host.

It is fairly common for a dog to become infected with an internal or external parasite at some point. Parasites can affect your furry friend in a variety of ways, ranging from simple irritation to causing life-threatening conditions if left untreated.

Some parasites can even infect and transmit diseases to you.

A zoonotic disease is a disease that can be passed directly or indirectly between animals and humans. Zoonotic diseases can be caused by viruses, bacteria, parasites and fungi.

Since humans interact with their furry friends on a daily basis, it's important to be aware of the different ways you can get zoonotic diseases. This can include coming into contact with the saliva, blood, urine or feces of an infected pet.

You can reduce the risk of parasite infection to you and your family by eliminating all parasites from your pets and restricting access to contaminated areas, such as sandboxes and high-traffic pet areas.

Remember to dispose of pet feces on a regular basis; it can help remove potentially infectious worm eggs before they become distributed in the environment and are picked up or ingested by pets or humans.

External parasites like fleas and ticks can affect your furry friend year-round.

Wildlife, including deer, coyotes, raccoons and skunks, can deposit flea eggs into a yard.

Remember, during the spring and summer months mow your lawn frequently; it reduces flea and tick hangouts. Neatness counts when it comes to eliminating habitats for fleas and ticks to hide and lay eggs. Remove yard debris, such as piles of lumber, bricks, and stones. Pick up discarded pots and other garden items; stack them neatly to limit refuge.

According to Sisters Veterinary Clinic in Central Oregon, there are more and more fleas and ticks invading pets year-round. Fleas and ticks can carry, and transmit directly or indirectly, several potential illnesses for humans. Bartonellosis is transmitted between cats by fleas, and then may spread to people. Fleas serve as an intermediate host for tapeworms, which can also infect both you and your pet.

Fleas are small, and just because you don't find one on your pet doesn't mean that they're not there and Rover isn't being bitten. Just a few fleas may not cause him to scratch, but they multiply fast.

Internal parasites like heartworms can be a very serious problem for both dogs and cats, especially those in mosquito-infested areas. Although heartworms are not a high risk in Sisters Country, if you travel with your pet to wetter areas, your furry friend can become infected.

Roundworms are one of the most common parasitic worms found inside cats and dogs. Both hookworms and roundworms can be transmitted to humans and can cause a variety of health problems. It is more likely with children who encounter a contaminated outdoor area.

Good hygiene wards off parasites. Wash your hands frequently and have your children do the same.

Any pet at any age can be infected with parasites, and your veterinarian can help prevent, accurately diagnose and safely treat parasites. It's important to implement a year-round parasite control program for your furry friends. It not only protects them, but it safeguards you and your family, too.

# So, you've decided to get a puppy

You've been talking about getting a dog for months. Your neighbor stops by to tell you that she has a big litter of 10-week-old puppies that need homes, just in case you're interested in one.

Since it's going to be your first dog, you've decided on a puppy. There's really nothing quite as endearing as a puppy. They're cute, cuddly and full of affection and the gaze from a pup's big round eyes can melt anyone's heart.

Bringing a new puppy into your home will also be a major lifestyle adjustment. Are you prepared?

Before you run down to the neighbor's house to take a look at those charming little fur balls, ponder a couple of pertinent questions first.

Do you have the time to dedicate to raising and training a puppy, and can you afford to take care of him?

You'll need to spend loads of time with baby Rover, because he requires constant supervision during his first months of life. If you had kids, you might remember the potty training sessions; it took patience and perseverance. Your pup will need the same. You've decided that the timing is right and adding a puppy would fit your lifestyle. You're ready for all the fun and challenging times that baby Rover will bring into your life.

Before you bring home your cute little furball, you need to puppy-proof your home. This process is similar to toddler-proofing a home. Get yourself down to his level and look around. Electrical cords, potential toxins, and breakable items should be placed out of reach. Remember your puppy can jump, climb, chew and scratch at things. Use child-safe latches for keeping poisons and other items out of reach. Although some pups are curious and determined enough to break the latches, so you may have to use metal hardware. Proper puppy-proofing not only keeps him safe, it also gives you peace of mind.

Before looking at a litter of puppies, remember you can't judge a puppy solely by its breed or looks. Don't let sudden infatuation make the decision for you. Consider whether you want a male or female. Often females are smaller in size, more submissive and less dominant. Males tend to be a little bit more independent. Take a good look at him for signs of physical problems, for instance; check that his eyes and nose are clear and clean and that his coat looks shiny.

Evaluating a pup's personality is also important. There's a good chance that a bright friendly puppy will grow up to be a bright friendly dog. Remember, the puppy that's cowering in the corner might end up a timid dog.

After two hours at the neighbor's house with oodles of playful puppies, you come to a decision. His quick friendly manner and the way he made eye contact with his big baby browns pulled on your heart strings and you knew.

Remember, baby Rover will need certain items from the very start and some are essential for your pup's well-being, like the right puppy food. Most important items include a leash and collar with identification, food and water bowls and chew toys. You should get a doggie bed and, preferably, a crate or kennel. Some of these items can last as your new furry friend ages, but bear in mind that most of them will need to be replaced as he grows.

One of the first things you and your new puppy should do together is go to the vet for his first checkup.

You should begin house-training as soon as you bring your new furry companion home; it can help to get him on a routine. As a general rule, you should take your puppy to the designated "potty spot" immediately after eating or drinking. Accidents do happen, so be prepared, consistent and patient. Beyond housebreaking, there are many more things you will need to teach your puppy. Start by working on socialization and leash training.

The bond you have with your puppy begins the moment he comes into your life and never stops growing. You can nurture this bond though affection, training, grooming, playtime, exercise and participation in various activities.

Remember, there is no crystal ball to know which puppy will grow into the best adult dog. A puppy is shaped into an adult by how it is trained and raised.

# More about puppy

When you first arrive home, your puppy may feel a little apprehensive and will be missing the companionship of her mom and littermates. To help make her transition stress-free, let your puppy explore her surroundings at her own pace. It's very important to supervise her at all times, even if you've puppy-proofed your home.

Kevin and Debbie Dyer, owners of Ponderosa Properties in Sisters, Oregon recently became pet parents to an eight-week-old Keeshond puppy. They have had Keeshonds before, but it's been a decade since they've raised one from puppyhood.

The Keeshond is an old dog breed, once a companion and watchdog on the barges and boats that traveled the canals and rivers of Holland in the $17^{th}$ and $18^{th}$ centuries, but almost exclusively a companion dog today. Keeshonds are people-lovers willing to participate in all family activities.

The Dyers' puppy, Gracie, came from a huge litter of 10 pups. This is their first female, and she chose them.

The first night in her new home, Gracie missed all her littermates. She had a nice comfortable bed of her own, but wasn't accustomed to her new surroundings yet. When Gracie cried, the Dyers took turns comforting her. And now, one month later at 12 weeks, she sleeps through the night. Gracie is being supervised at all times by her pet parents, but they found that she can run off lickety-split.

While everyone's lifestyle is different, try to put together a consistent schedule for you and your puppy to follow. Consistency and routine will work in your favor, and your puppy's, when it comes to reliable housebreaking, nap times and play times.

The Dyers are consistent pet parents, and Gracie is on a daily routine. Since puppies have small stomachs and need to eat small portions three or four times a day. Gracie eats breakfast, lunch and dinner the same time each day.

Within a few days of taking your new puppy home, you should bring her to your veterinarian for a general exam and to start on vaccinations. Your vet can help identify any potential health issues early on, and advise you on caring for your puppy long-term.

Gracie had her health checkup and is now on the second round of vaccinations.

Housebreaking is one of the first things you will teach your new puppy. This process can sometimes be quite difficult, though some puppies catch on earlier than others. You should begin house-training as soon as you bring your puppy home, but it takes patience. Puppies are generally not able to control their bladders and bowels until about 12 weeks of age. If your puppy is younger than this, please be patient. Starting early can help get your puppy on a routine.

Gracie began learning to go potty outside right away, every two hours to begin with, and as she matured, she could go longer without an accident. At 12 weeks, Gracie is almost completely housebroken thanks to consistency, and being carefully monitored at all times.

Although it's essential to consistently supervise your puppy during the house-training process, there's bound to be a time when you must leave her home alone for a few hours. Walk your puppy about one hour before leaving her alone. Take her outside so she can go potty and play a game of fetch or chase to get any excess energy out before you leave. Or you might recruit a puppy-sitter to stay with her for those few hours.

The Dyers have decided not to leave Gracie alone just yet. She goes to work with them every day at Ponderosa Properties. Gracie is also being socialized while spending time at work with her pet parents. Right now the Dyers' schedule is wrapped around Gracie's needs.

The bond you have with your puppy begins the moment he comes into your life and never stops growing. You can nurture this bond through affection, training, grooming, playtime, general exercise and participation in various activities. It's important to spend quality time with your puppy, and though your daily routine will normally be a few walks, and some play, why not make things exciting on occasion by going on an adventure?

Gracie goes on walks and loves to play outside; she enjoys meeting new people wherever she goes. So far one of Gracie's favorite experiences is going to Hoodoo and sliding down a snowy hill on her belly.

Chewing is a very normal behavior for puppies and dogs of all ages. They do it out of pleasure, to relieve stress and to exercise their jaws and teeth. It is your responsibility as a pet parent to provide her with the things she can chew on, like her own special chew toys.

Gracie has a toy-box full of toys to play with and to chew on. The Dyers know how natural it is for puppies to want to chew. It's all about re-directing your puppy to chew what she is supposed to rather than the leg of your couch.

Becoming a new pet parent can be an extremely rewarding experience, but it also carries with it responsibility. A new puppy will become part of the family for her life and you will be responsible for her well-being.

# Coping with the loss of a pet

Our pets bring so much love, support, and companionship into our lives. Many people have experienced the joy that comes with having a pet, yet sadly there also comes a time when they have to face the heartbreak of losing that cherished friend.

A pet is a constant companion, and facing its loss can be devastating.

Given the intense bond most of us share with our animals, it's natural to feel overwhelmed by feelings of grief when a pet dies. For many people a pet is not "just a dog" or "just a cat." Pets are beloved members of the family and when they pass away, you may feel a significant, traumatic loss.

Grieving is a personal, individual experience. Some people find the mourning process comes in stages, where they experience different feelings such as denial, anger, guilt, depression, and eventually acceptance. Others find that grief may come in waves, or a series of highs and lows. Some people may take weeks to sort out their sadness, while others can take months or even years. Your age, how the pet passed away and the closeness of your relationship all play a part in the feelings you experience.

Give yourself permission to grieve. Accept the fact that you were very close to your pet and recognize how much your animal friend meant to you.

Stay connected with friends. Seek out people who will let you express your sorrow. A warm understanding and supportive listener can help tremendously.

Memorialize your pet, planting a tree in his memory, or start a scrapbook to share the memories you enjoyed with your pet with family members and friends.

Pets' help many adults stay active and playful, which can boost your immune system and increase your energy. It's important to keep up your activity levels after the loss of your pet.

Surviving pets can also experience loss when another animal in the household dies, or they may become distressed by your sorrow. Maintaining their daily routines, or even increasing exercise and play times will not only benefit the surviving pets but may also elevate your outlook, too.

When the family pet dies, children can also have a hard time coming to terms with this loss. For many children, the loss of a pet may be their first experience with death.

You can explain to your child that the pet lives on in memories and answer any questions your child may have. You can also explain that it is normal for them to feel really sad for awhile. Photos of your pet may also be of comfort to your child.

While grief is a personal experience, you don't need to face your loss alone. Many forms of support are available, including pet-bereavement counseling services, pet-loss support hotlines, and local or online pet-bereavement groups. By calling a local humane society you can find out whether it offers a pet-loss support group or can refer you to one.

Working through your grief will help you to get closer to the day when you are able to remember your pet with a smile. While you'll always miss your pet, time does dull the pain and heal your grief.

# Dogs riding in pickup trucks

It may be convenient to load your dog up in the back of your truck and take them with you, but carrying dogs in open pickup beds poses a threat to both your pet and other motorists.

Dogs riding in the back of trucks might look like they are having fun. They get to go somewhere with their owner, after all. But what if you hit a bump or swerve to avoid an obstacle? Your dog could easily fly out of the truck.

Imagine slamming on the brakes while your precious dog is in the truck bed. We're safe because we wear seatbelts. Not so for your dog.

According to the Humane Society of the United States, 100,000 dogs are killed each year in accidents involving riding in truck beds.

Sana Hayes, Brightside Animal Center volunteer program coordinator in Redmond, Oregon remembers a tragic accident involving a dog in the back of a truck.

"Years ago I was in my car behind a pickup carrying a German shepherd. The truck swerved and the dog was thrown from the truck and killed by another vehicle. It was traumatic."

Oregon Revised Statute 811.200 prohibits carrying a dog on an external part of a vehicle unless the dog is protected by framework, carrier, or other device to keep the dog from falling from the vehicle. This offense is considered a Class D violation.

Sergeant Troy Gotchy of the Deschutes County Sheriff's office knows that it's not illegal in Oregon to have your dog in the back of a framed pickup - but he wouldn't do it himself.

"I would personally not allow my dog to run free in the back of a truck on the road," he said. "It's not a safe thing to do. He could easily jump or be thrown out."

There are more problems for dogs riding in the back of pickups than being thrown out.

Being in the open air traveling at high speeds can cause damage to the delicate parts of their face. Wind is a painful hazard. Wind whipping through the dog's ears is full of dirt, debris, and gravel that can lodge in the eyes, nose, or ears and cause serious damage.

Tying the dog to the truck bed can be dangerous, too. Ropes and leashes become nooses if the dog should be jolted out of the truck

Veterinarians see numerous cases of dogs being injured because they jumped out or were thrown from the bed of a pickup truck. If these dogs are lucky enough to still be alive, broken legs and joint injuries are among the most common types of damage that they sustain, and often result in amputation.

The best solution is to let them ride in the cab with you or leave them at home.

Your dog might enjoy the trip much more if he doesn't have to fight against gravity, jolts, and wind to get there.

"Dogs don't have hands to be able to hold onto something while in the back of a truck. I think of it like a dog being in a slippery bathtub and cannot hold on," says Hayes.

If you must take them with you in the back of a pickup, best practice is to use a secured crate or place a canopy over the bed.

# Could you be allergic to your pet?

You've recently bonded with your rescue dog after working for weeks on training and socializing him. You've noticed that your allergies seem much worse and it's not even spring. Could it be your furry friend?

One of the worst discoveries pet parents can make is that they are (or a family member is) allergic to a four-legged family member.

Some people develop an immune reaction to a certain protein produced in the sebaceous glands of a dog or cat's skin. This allergen is found in the animal's dander; the tiny scales of dead skin that pets are constantly shedding. Allergens are also present in a dog or cat's saliva and urine. Your pet secrets fluids and sheds the dander that contains the allergens. They collect on fur and other surfaces and can get onto everything.

If you suspect you're allergic to your four-legged friend, it is important to see an allergist and be tested.

According to the Humane Society of the United States, studies show that approximately 15 percent of the population is allergic to dogs or cats. In a study of 341 adults who were allergic to cats or dogs and had been advised by their doctors to give up their pets, only one in five did. It's clear the benefits of pet companionship outweigh the drawbacks of pet allergies for many owners.

However, some people believe that once they are diagnosed with a pet allergy, they have no choice but to remove their furry friend from their home.

Thankfully, there are many solutions that can be explored that would allow an allergy sufferer to keep their four-legged family member while successfully managing their allergies - as long as the allergies are just a nuisance, but are non-life-threatening. They can choose to live with Rover or Kitty by modifying behaviors and keeping the house as dander-free as possible.

Keeping a clean house helps combat allergies. Clean your home frequently and thoroughly to remove dust and dander (wear a mask if you're the one allergic). Use a vacuum with high-efficiency particulate air, or HEPA filtration. HEPA purifiers can theoretically remove at least 99.97 percent of dust, pollen, mold, dander, and other airborne particles.

Clean pet beds, rugs, and blankets as often as possible. Use cleaning products that pick up and hold dust and dirt, such as microfiber cloths. Sticky rollers work great for picking up pet hair off couches, chairs and beds, but having washable covers works even better.

Use HEPA room air purifiers throughout your home to keep dander under control. Avoid dust- and dander-catching furnishings such as cloth curtains and carpeted floors. If you are able, remove carpets and use tile or other non-carpeted flooring.

High-efficiency air filters should be used in your home's heating and air-conditioning systems.

Create an "allergy-free" zone in your home by making the allergic family member's bedroom strictly off-limits to those with four paws, and place a HEPA air purifier in the room.

Make it a petty crime when Rover jumps up on the furniture - but please provide him with a nice bed to call his own. If Rover's bed is washable, wash it weekly using hot water.

Brushing and bathing your furry friend on a weekly basis can reduce the level of allergy-causing dander. Even cats can become accustomed to being bathed.

Immunology (allergy shots) can improve symptoms but cannot eliminate them entirely. They work by gradually desensitizing a person's immune system to the pet allergens. Immunology has been used successfully for more than 100 years, and can help people with serious allergies that might otherwise have to give up their furry friends.

Additional treatments for allergies to pets are symptomatic, including steroidal and antihistamine nose sprays and antihistamine pills. There are multiple over-the-counter medications out there. Check with your doctor first to find the one that fits your needs best.

There are combinations of solutions that can control your pet allergies and hopefully work for you. There are a large number of animal-lovers who manage their allergies and live happily and healthily with their four-legged family members.

# What emotions do dogs feel?

You've caught the flu and you really feel poorly. Rover watches your every move and won't leave your side all day, which is out of the norm for him. Could he be feeling empathy?

Two recent studies are moving us closer than ever to a definite answer. In a UK study, two researchers at Goldsmiths College in London, Deborah Custance and Jennifer Mayer, set out to determine if dogs are capable of empathy. They designed a clever experiment to test whether a dog's behavior around apparently distressed people is consistent with empathy.

First they gathered a group of largely untrained dogs, mostly mixed breeds of both males and females. Then they set up a situation with the dog's pet parent and a stranger to the pooch. The pet parent and the stranger would alternately talk, cry, or hum a song.

The researchers wanted to see how the dogs reacted. If the dogs felt empathy, they would be more likely to approach whoever was crying. The intervals of talking provided a baseline because low key human conversation is something that happens around dogs all the time, and that isn't usually much interest to them.

The dogs responded: 15 of the 18 in the study sought out the person in distress even if that person was the stranger.

"On the surface, it certainly seemed as if the dogs were demonstrating empathy," said Custance, who thought that if the dogs were seeking comfort for themselves they would go to their pet parent.

She admitted that the study raises other questions: What about other emotions, such as pleasure or anger?

There's no doubt that dogs have emotions. They feel joy after a job well done, and they feel sadness when another furry family member passes away.

Dogs even have the hormone oxytocin, which in humans is involved with feeling love and affection for others.

Most people routinely read emotions in their furry friends: a wagging tail when you arrive home means Rover's happy, or if his ears are back and he's crouching low to the ground with his tail tucked under, he's fearful. Another example could be when you're out on a walk and when another canine approaches, Rover freezes in place, his hackles raised, and he gives a low throaty growl, at that point, you probably realize that your furry friend does not like the other dog, and he is angry.

However, it's important to remember that those emotions are different from those of adult humans. The feeling that dogs experience isn't connected to complex thoughts. Studies say they don't have ulterior motives or doubt. Their emotions are pure and honest.

Researchers have now come to believe that the mind of a dog is compared to that of a human who is two to two-and-a-half years old. The researchers' conclusion holds for most mental abilities as well as emotions.

Dogs seem to have an intuitive understanding of fair play, and become resentful if they feel that another dog is getting a better deal, a new study has found. The study found that dogs are capable of feeling jealous or of judging fairness.

Friederike Range, a researcher at the University of Vienna in Austria, and her colleagues did a series of experiments that show that dogs will stop doing a simple task when not rewarded if another dog continues to be rewarded.

The experiment consisted of taking pairs of dogs and getting them to give a paw for a reward. On giving this "handshake" the dogs received a piece of food.

The dogs were normally happy to repeatedly give the paw, whether they got a reward or not.

But that all changed if they saw that another dog was being rewarded with a piece of food, while they received nothing.

The dog without the reward quickly stopped doing the task, and showed signs of annoyance or stress when its partner was rewarded.

"Dogs show a strong aversion to unfairness," said Dr. Range, who conducted the study.

So what does this mean for people who live and interact with their furry friends?

The good news is that you can still feel free to dress your pooch in that silly costume for the Halloween parade, and he will not feel shame, regardless of how silly he might look. Your dog will also not feel pride at taking home the top prize in the talent contest. But your dog can consistently feel love for you and feel contentment from your company, and that's really the heart of the matter.

# Dog friendships

Your furry friend has become a good play buddy with Sparky, your sister's dog. Each time Sparky comes to visit they play chase and romp around the yard for an hour until they are both exhausted from their fun interaction.

Just like us, dogs are social animals, and many enjoy spending time with each other. Remember that they are descendants of wolves, who ran in packs.

They enjoy interacting with people, other dogs and yes, even other species, such as cats and farm animals. But just as humans relate better to another human, so will a dog relate better to another dog. Your furry friend can form a fast friendship with another dog, or he can take an instant dislike to another dog, just like we do with the people we meet.

If your pooch is a social butterfly that seems happy rather than afraid or aggressive when hanging around with other dogs, it's a great idea to give him regular opportunities to play and romp with his canine buddies.

Play with other dogs helps keep Rover's socialization skills polished, wears him out mentally, tires him out physically, and is a lot of fun.

Dogs learn from each other, and they can form strong friendship bonds with other dogs. Allowing Rover the freedom to choose some canine friends is just good pet parenting.

Animal behaviorists agree that dogs need environmental stimulation, just like humans.

Stanley Cohen, Ph.D., in an article for Psychology Today said: "In the thousands of years since humans first domesticated dogs, we have genetically manipulated them to socialize easily and to show friendliness almost indiscriminately. Dogs that have been properly socialized will happily approach virtually any animal, regardless of its species, and unless they receive hostile signals, they will attempt to establish a good-natured relationship."

It's wonderful to watch two dogs running around together, wrestling and chasing each other, but not all dogs enjoy playing with other canines.

Some might fear or dislike other dogs because they didn't get socialized enough during puppyhood, and some dogs who enjoyed playing with canine companions as puppies, might rather relax by themselves as older adults. Some dogs simply seem to prefer the company of humans. So before you try to find friends for your furry friend, make sure he truly seems to want playmates.

Take Rover on walks and watch his body language when he sees or meets other dogs. You can usually tell if your furry friend wants to interact with another dog. He might whine or bark with excitement, bounce around wagging his tail and play bow (lower his front end while keeping his rear in the air) and of course he will want to circle and sniff the other dog.

You can also tell when he'd rather not interact, he might try to avoid the other dog, become stiff and tense looking, show his teeth, growl, snap, cower, tremble or even try to hide behind you.

If you notice that your pooch is really friendly around other dogs, there are several options for finding him playmates, such as dog parks and doggie daycares. If you have friends or family with dogs, you can arrange "play dates" at home. You can also look for playmates while on walks in public places. If you and your dog frequent a local park, for example, you'll likely see other dogs and their pet parents on a regular basis. So if your pooch repeatedly meets and likes another dog, consider arranging some off-leash play in a safe, enclosed area, such as your fenced yard.

If you have a puppy, it's important for him to have plenty of socialization with other puppies, but it's also crucial for him to learn how to interact with older dogs, too. Enrolling your little furry friend in a puppy class that includes off-leash playtime might be a good start.

Many dogs learn to play gently with smaller or more delicate friends. However, it's best to seek similar-sized playmates for your dog.

Above all, pay attention to what your pooch wants. When you introduce him to potential pals, notice which ones he seems most excited to see, and which ones he plays with the longest. If Rover consistently ignores another dog or tries to stop play by leaving the area, hiding or growling, listen to what he's saying. He might prefer another playmate.

# Dogs and cats: Learning to get along together

Can cats and dogs get along? While there have been many movies that had fun with the idea that the animals are secretly fighting an all-out war, many real-life cats and dogs live in harmony together in the same household.

It is important to understand how cats' and dogs' personalities vary. One of the biggest differences between canines and felines lies in their social patterns and interactions. Cats tend to be solitary animals, preferring to go where they want when they want, and ask for attention at their discretion. Dogs on the other hand are pack animals and the members of their pack or family are vital to them. Dogs value time spent with and close to their pack or family.

Getting a dog and cat to accept one another can be difficult, as anyone who's tried to introduce them knows. There are a few basic steps to getting both pets to call an inter-species truce.

The key to a successful first encounter is slow and controlled introductions. Be alert for potential problems so you can avoid or minimize them. You want to create a positive association about the other, so keep lots of treats nearby. Regardless of whether you are getting a new cat or a new dog, the first introduction between your current pet and your new pet is a very important part of the process.

If you have a dog and are planning to bring a cat into the household, start working on your pooch's obedience before you add your new pet. Rover should be comfortable on a leash, and trained well enough to mind your requests while on a leash.

If you have a cat in the household and are planning to bring in a dog, create a place your cat can retreat to, preferably high off the ground, which the dog cannot reach or climb to. Move the litter box and food and water dishes to a location the dog will not be able to access.

One way for Rover and your feline to get used to each other over the first few days is to rotate which animal has freedom and which is confined, to allow each animal time to investigate the other's scent. Sometimes your pooch should be confined to a crate or another room (or taken to another location if she can't be left alone) to allow your cat time to roam free and investigate the smell of your dog.

For the first face-to-face introduction, make sure your dog is securely leashed. When both pets are behaving calmly (could be awhile) try dropping the leash, but stay nearby and grab the leash if you have to. Unless your dog and cat enjoy each other's company right away and want to harmlessly play with each other (could happen with a friendly kitten and puppy), keep the dog on a leash for a couple of weeks in the cat's presence, and make sure your cat has a way to escape from your pooch.

Don't force interaction and have plenty of treats around for rewarding good behavior.

Unsupervised time together should occur only when your household is consistently incident-free.

One way to get better results in that first introduction is to adopt from a local shelter or rescue group; they can help you find that special dog-friendly cat or cat-loving dog.

When it works, there is nothing sweeter than seeing how a little kitten can hold a big old dog around her dainty little paw - or how a tough, battle-scarred veteran cat will melt at a puppy's charms.

It's not uncommon for dogs and cats to become friends and to enjoy each other's company. Just by taking the time to manage your cat-dog introduction properly, you could be setting up a friendship that will last for the rest of your furry friends' life.

Good luck!

# Sniffing out disease

Any pet parent can tell you: pets are amazing. They're loyal, comfort us in tough times, and even lower a person's blood pressure.

Some animals seem to perform what seem like miracles, attracting attention for rescuing their pet parents from dangerous situations or predicting health problems before they occur, such as alerting humans to changes in their blood pressure.

And anyone who has ever spent time with a dog knows that dogs love sniffing! They sniff out hidden food, dirty socks, and the visitor who comes to the door. Some dogs work with police officers, soldiers and even scientists to put their "sniffers" to work.

Due to their superior sense of smell, dogs can smell in parts per trillion. For example, if you diluted less than a drop of blood into 20 Olympic-sized swimming pools, a dog would know that there was blood in the pool. Dogs smell like we see. We walk into a room and see the room; the dog sees it through his nose.

Dogs have been trained to sniff gunpowder, narcotics, missing persons, and now diseases.

Dogs' remarkable ability to sniff out disease is opening doors to earlier cancer detection and better understanding of the disease process itself.

Just the word cancer puts us in fear. It is an uncontrolled division of abnormal cells that destroy nearby healthy tissue.

Infectious diseases such as cholera, diphtheria, smallpox, pneumonia, tuberculosis, typhoid fever and yellow fever have long been known to produce signature odors.

Cancer also has an odor, and researchers now know one thing for sure: dogs can smell cancer.

Dogs are up front about this smelling stuff, greeting each other with a thorough sniff from tip to tail, quickly gathering a wealth of information through their noses.

Did you ever notice how your pooch shows intense interest in a new cut on your arm or leg?

They are inhaling volatile organic compounds, or VOCs. VOCs are chemicals coming from a living or once-living organism that can pass into the surrounding air. (Volatile means easily evaporated at normal temperatures.) A human body constantly emits an incredible variety of VOCs, some that are odorous and some that are not.

Most oncologists will tell you that humans can actually smell cancer in later stages through the patient's breath. If humans can pick up the odor in later stages, then of course a dog would be able to detect it in a human much earlier.

There are many published studies that prove dogs can detect cancer through breath samples.

Cancer has been the most recent focus of this sort of research. The earlier cancer is detected, the better the patient's chances are for survival. Dogs can detect certain cancers with high levels of accuracy long before some of the more traditional diagnostic methods.

The trick is identifying the signature VOC that relates to a specific type of cancer so that the dog can be trained to alert to it. Researchers are making great progress. Dogs have been trained to detect ovarian cancer in blood samples - distinguishing it from other gynecological cancers and from healthy samples.

Researchers from the Italian Ministry of Defense Military Veterinary Center in Grosseto were able to train two German shepherds, Liu and Zoey, to sniff out VOCs associated with prostate cancer in urine samples with 98 percent accuracy. The study was presented at the American Urological Association annual meeting.

Training dogs to smell cancer is done in the same way that bomb and narcotics dogs are trained, pairing the target odor with a high-value reward.

Dr. George Preti, a chemist at the Monell Chemical Senses Center in Philadelphia, has spent much of his career trying to isolate the volatile chemicals behind cancer's unique odor. He is working to isolate the chemical biomarkers responsible for ovarian cancers subtle smell using high-tech spectrometers and chromatographs. Once he identifies that compound, he will test whether dogs will respond to that chemical in the same way they respond to the actual ovarian cancer smell.

"I'm not embarrassed to say that a dog is better than my instruments," Dr. Preti said.

So the next step will be to build a mechanical, hand-held sensor or an electronic nose that can detect that cancer chemical in the clinic.

And this is all possible because of man's best friend - the dog!

# Dogs and their toys

You return home after being gone for a few hours. Rover is at the door to greet you wagging his tail with "Squiggles," his favorite rubber squeak toy, clenched between his teeth, ready to play.

Dogs play, snuggle, and sleep with their toys; some even bury their toys. Toys are important for puppies and young dogs. Dogs that have toys to play with are less bored. Often, dogs that have behavior problems have lots of energy and nothing to do. Toys can direct your furry friend to healthy behaviors, use up excess energy, and be a way for the two of you to play together. Playing with different toys encourages exercise, which benefits your pet's overall health.

Deciding what toy to buy for your restless pooch isn't an easy decision. Each dog has a unique personality and energy level, and therefore will have a unique preference for the type of toy he likes to play with. There are chew toys, rubber toys, ropes, tug toys, balls, stuffed toys and food dispensing toys.

Toys keep dogs busy. Some are useful when pet parents cannot play with their dogs, like food puzzle toys and dental chew toys.

Dog toys are not safe if small pieces can be chewed or pulled off, as these could be swallowed by your furry friend. Choose toys made with non-toxic materials. Educate yourself before buying toys for Rover. Read the warning and size/weight labels. Many factors contribute to the safety or danger of a toy, and a number of them depend upon your dog's size, activity level, and preferences. The size and aggression of the dog will help you determine what to get. Dogs, like children, have oral fixations, so everything goes in their mouths.

There are a wide variety of dog toys on the market that are designed for different purposes, depending on your furry friend's characteristics.

Be cautious, because the things that are usually most attractive to dogs are often the very things that are the most dangerous. Dog-proof your home by removing ribbon, rubber bands, human children's toys and anything else that Rover can get his mouth on and be ingested. Toys should be appropriate for your dog's size.

The urge to chew is deeply ingrained in your dog's instincts, so finding the right toy is important, especially if your pooch tends to want to chew on your table legs. If you are a pet parent to a puppy, there is no getting around the fact that baby Rover will need to chew (teething) and you can guide him toward constructive chewing with the right toy.

Most dog trainers prefer using Kong toys, which come in different sizes and are made of hard rubber. Some of the Kong toys are also food-dispenser toys. Nylabones can also be good for chewing. With the right chew toy, dogs that are aggressive chewers have a safe way to satisfy their biting instincts. If you're thinking of giving your pooch rawhide chew toys, be sure to check with your veterinarian about which ones are safe and appropriate for your dog.

Tennis balls are great for fetch, but not for chewing on because they can come apart and be ingested. Balls of all shapes and sizes help keep dogs active and fit; they are a great way to play and exercise a dog at the same time. The flying disc or Frisbee is also fun for Rover and will keep him fit, but you don't want it to be so tough that it could hurt your pooch's teeth or mouth if he doesn't catch it perfectly.

Most dogs enjoy playing tug-of-war, and rope toys are usually available in a "bone" shape with knotted ends.

Your pooch might like comfort toys or "stuffies," soft toys that are good for several purposes, but aren't appropriate for all dogs. Depending on Rover's size, the stuffed toy should be small enough to carry around, but not too small to choke on.

Pay attention to any toy that contains a squeaker buried in the center; your pooch may feel that he must find and destroy the source of the squeaking, and he could end up swallowing it.

There are many toys that Rover would have a great time with by himself or interacting with you. Remember to educate yourself about the kind of toys that you think would be best for your particular dog. It's also important to remember that all toys can pose a risk if your dog ingests them, so play should be supervised, especially with aggressive chewers.

# Fun and easy tricks for your dog

Tricks build relationships. When you sit on the floor and teach your furry friend to chase after a toy and bring it back, you are training a fun and useful trick. Perhaps more importantly, you are also being part of one of the key human-dog bonding behaviors: Play! When we have fun with our dogs, our bond grows.

Dog tricks are also a great way to offer your dog some mental stimulation, and it gives you another way of interacting with him. Plus, it's a lot of fun to train your pooch to do some cool dog tricks to show off for friends or a Dog Talent Contest!

When most people think of dog training, they think of the basic dog training commands - sit, down, come, stay. While those basic obedience essentials are important, don't underestimate the benefits of training your

Jodi Schneider McNamee

furry friend to do tricks. Hopefully your pooch already knows a few basic commands, but if he doesn't he can learn easy enough; it just takes a little time and patience on your part.

Here is an example of teaching a basic training command:

"Sit" is usually one of the first things folks teach their dogs, and is part of basic obedience training. The "sit" is very easy to teach. Just hold a tasty treat in your hand just in front of Fido's nose and allow him to smell it but not eat it. Very slowly bring the treat up and back over his head; as his nose comes up following the treat, his back end will lower until he's sitting. Once he's sitting, praise him by saying "good" or whatever word works for you, and reward him.

Here are some dog tricks that are fun and fairly easy to train a dog to do:

Back-up is a fun dog trick that can come in quite handy. It's useful if you need your dog to back away from an open door, back away from you when he's crowding you during a game of fetch, or if you simply want to impress your friends.

You don't need any special equipment to train your dog to back up. As long as you have your pooch and a handful of treats, you are ready to go.

Start off by giving your dog the "stay" command. If your dog doesn't know how to stay yet, it would help if you went back and worked on that before moving on to the next step.

Take a few steps away from your dog, and then turn and face him. Give your dog the command "back up," and then begin moving towards him.

Some dogs will take a few steps back the minute you start moving in their direction. If your dog doesn't start stepping back as you move toward him, keep going forward, and try to lean your body forward slightly.

As soon as your dog takes a few steps back, tell him "good" and give him a treat.

Most dogs learn to back up quickly. Practice the steps above for a few minutes each day, and your dog will soon be responding to the backup command.

Taking a bow is a cool dog trick, and the perfect finishing touch when showing off your dog's tricks. All you need to train your dog to take a bow is your dog and some treats.

Start with your dog standing up. Hold a treat at the tip of your dog's nose, and slowly move it down, holding it close to your dog's body. In this way, you will use the treat to lure your dog down until his elbows are on the floor with his rear end remaining up.

Hold your dog in the bow for a few seconds, and then use the treat to lure him back into a standing position. As soon as your dog completes the bow and is standing up, tell him "good" and give him the treat.

Practice the bow command with your dog several times a day for no more than five minutes each time. Before you know it, your dog will be taking a bow on command.

Begging is another cute dog trick that is moderately easy to train your furry friend to do.

Have a handful of your dog's favorite treats ready when you begin training him to beg.

Start training your dog to do this trick by asking him to sit. With your pooch in a sitting position, hold a treat at his nose, and give him the command "beg."

As your dog reaches to take the treat in his mouth, slowly raise the treat over his head so that he'll have to reach up to get it.

Pull it up until he is sitting on his hind end with his paws off the floor, and held in front of him in the begging position.

Whichever trick you try with your furry friend, remember it is all about interaction and fun.

# Finding the right vet for your pet

You've just adopted a four month-old puppy from the local humane society. There's a lot to learn about your new furry friend, and one of the most important decisions you'll make as a pet parent is finding a quality health-care provider for him.

When you bring a new pet into your life, you are responsible from that day forward for his care, which includes nutrition, safety and health.

Selecting the right veterinarian is a personal decision, but you'll want to choose a practice that offers the highest available care, one that you can trust to care for your pet's health through the years.

Your veterinarian is one of your pet's most important caretakers. So finding and establishing a relationship with the right vet can be critical to the long-term health and well-being of your cat or dog. Whether you're new to pet parenting or need to switch vets, here are some helpful tips to consider during your search.

Start by asking friends, family or neighbors - preferably those who own a dog or cat, for recommendations. But chances are if you purchased your pet from a local breeder or animal shelter, they would know the local vet community and can refer you to a trusted practice.

Always be sure to double-check references.

The American Animal Hospital Association (AAHA) evaluates veterinary practices on the quality of their facilities, staff, equipment and patient care. So you can search the organization's website at www.healthypet.com for a list of accredited vets in your area.

And if possible choose a vet that is close to home. Short car rides will help minimize stress to your dog or cat, especially if he is sick or injured.

When selecting a vet, you're doing more than searching for a medical expert. You're looking for someone to meet your needs and those of your pet, a doctor who has people as well as animal skills.

Remember, the worst time to look for a vet is when you really need on, so plan ahead and choose wisely.

Once you've narrowed your search, schedule a visit to meet the staff and tour the facility to learn about the hospitals philosophy and policies. This really is a reasonable request that any vet should be glad to do, so don't be shy. Write down your questions ahead of time.

A few things you should look for when touring the facility are cleanliness, friendliness and organization.

Since veterinarians often work with a team of professionals, including technicians and qualified support staff, you might want to evaluate the vet's team's competence.

Is the staff calm, courteous and caring, and do they communicate effectively?

Remember to consider the hospital's location and think about fees when making a decision.

A good hospital should have access to x-ray, ultrasound, dentistry, in-house lab tests, IV pumps, blood-pressure, and eye-pressure monitoring, as well as the ability to send out labs and refer to specialists. This is important to know because if your pet ends up with an emergency, the quicker he gets care, the better. It will help you feel more comfortable to be able to know that your vet's hospital is equipped with whatever Rover or Kitty needs for urgent care.

Schedule a "get-to-know-you" wellness appointment. Making a wellness appointment at a time when your pet is otherwise healthy is a great way to get to know your new vet, facility, and staff.

The first staff member you usually meet is a veterinarian technician or assistant. Does the staff member seem knowledgeable about and sensitive to your pet?

After your new vet enters the exam room, observe how he or she interacts with your furry friend. The vet should approach your pet in a friendly manner to minimize stress and provide positive interaction.

The vet should smile and be upbeat during the routine wellness call and shouldn't be in a hurry and attempt to speed up the exam.

Remember that appointments will go more smoothly when you have a list of questions to ask your vet.

Once you've found the right vet for you and your furry friend, have regular preventative visits, not just when Rover or Kitty becomes ill.

Learn what's normal for your pet, so you recognize the first signs of illness. If your pet's not well, don't wait until he's really sick before you call your vet.

# Halloween safety tips for pets

Halloween can be a fun and festive time for children and families - but for pets it can be a downright nightmare. For all the fun it offers for kids, Halloween can be unsettling and even dangerous for pets. Here are some common-sense precautions to keep in mind for your furry friend's safety this weekend.

Not only will your door be constantly opening and closing on Halloween, but ghosts and goblins intending to look scary that come to your door may actually be frightening to your pet. Your pet doesn't understand why so many masked or creepy creatures are heading to their home, and these costumed kids will be full of energy and yelling out for candy. This, of course, is scary for your four-legged family members.

Redmond Humane Society, Executive Director Chris Bauersfeld reveals her concerns about pets and Halloween.

"Pets are protective of their home and can get freaked out when kids are in costumes. It's a prime time when dogs and cats can get out of their house with all the restless anxious energy that they feel right before Halloween. Kids get very excited around Halloween and animals sense this. Dogs are especially territorial and may become anxious and growl at trick-or-treaters," Bauersfeld says.

Pets may do unpredictable things when they're scared, so keep them tucked away in a quiet and safe room on Halloween. Even if your pets are used to being outdoors, keep them indoors on Halloween night - especially black cats.

Black cats have long served as objects of superstition. They were considered bringers of bad luck and curses to any human they came near, and were associated with witchcraft. For years there have been concerns - though it's based on little more than hearsay - that black cats are sought out on Halloween and can be at risk from pranksters.

During the week of Halloween, calls to the veterinarians at Pet Poison Helpline increase by 12 percent. Most of the calls involve dogs' accidently ingesting candy. Of all candy, chocolate is one of the most toxic to pets. Many dogs are attracted to the smell and taste of chocolate, making it a significant threat. Some candies contain the artificial sweetener xylitol, and it can also be poisonous to pets, so keep Halloween candy well out of the reach of pets at all times.

Halloween decorations such as candles and jack-o'-lanterns can also be a hazard when they are within your dog or cat's range. Wagging tails and frightened cats zooming through the house can easily tip over a candle or carved pumpkin, causing burns or a fire.

Always make sure your dog or cat has proper identification. If for any reason your pet escapes and becomes lost, a collar and tags can be a lifesaver, increasing the chances that he will be returned to you.

"It's basic advice, but we tend to forget that it could be really dangerous for our pets with all the excitement in the air, let's keep them safe," said Bauersfeld.

Do not hesitate to contact your veterinarian or the 24-hour Pet Poison Helpline immediately at 1-800-213-6680 if you suspect that your furry friend has ingested something or might be injured.

# Heat can be deadly for your pet

A torrid heatwave has shifted into high gear. It broke at least seven June record highs in the Northwest, and weather forecasts indicate that it will extend through early July.

When temperatures soar, it is important to keep your pet in mind when it comes to keeping cool.

Summertime may be the time for walking and playing in the sunshine with Rover, but unfortunately your furry friend has a much harder time keeping cool than you, especially when temperatures are on the rise.

Be mindful of the heat and keep your dog cool to protect him from heat-related illness and injury. Heatstroke in dogs is a potential killer - but it is easy to avoid.

Leaving your pet in a parked car can be a deadly mistake. The temperature inside a car can reach 120 degrees in a few minutes. Even partially open windows won't protect your furry friend from heatstroke!

## PARKED CARS ARE DEATHTRAPS FOR DOGS.

While people can identify signs of exhaustion or stress, it can be harder to determine when pets are distressed. According to Oregon Humane Society, excessive thirst, heavy panting, lethargy, drooling, vomiting and an internal temperature of 104 degrees are all signs of heat stress.

Karen Burns, shelter manager for the Humane Society of Central Oregon (HSCO), warns people to keep their pets safe from the dangers of warm temperatures. According to Burns, every year HSCO hears about dogs needlessly suffering from heat stroke, and the City of Bend Animal Control receives four to eight calls per day regarding dogs left in hot cars during the summer months.

Heatstroke or exhaustion can occur very quickly for your pooch as he only has the ability to sweat through the pads of his feet. And the way Rover expels heat is through panting.

Remember that your furry friend doesn't realize that he will overheat while playing fetch in the park on a hot day; he won't know when he is overheated until it is too late. It's up to you as a responsible pet parent to watch for heat stress and dehydration in your dog, know when it's time to take a break, to give him a drink, and to rest in the shade for a while.

The best time to exercise your furry friend in the summer heat is early in the morning or later in the evening. Since these are the cooler parts of the day, this will make the walk more comfortable for both you and Rover.

Remember to keep your pooch hydrated.

Different dogs have different needs when battling the heat. Keep in mind that dogs with darker coats absorb more heat than lighter coats.

Also overweight dogs, very young or older dogs are at a higher risk for dehydration. Carry a bottle of water when going on a walk with your furry friend.

Get creative and find innovative ways to cool Rover down. Find a spot in the shade and set up a kiddie pool. Lay down a wet towel for your dog to lie on or let him run through the sprinklers.

Did you know that dogs cool from the bottom up? So make sure to spray the paws and stomach, not just the top of Fido. That's why a wet towel does more good on the bottom of your dog than when laid on top of him.

If you walk your furry friend on the roadside you might need doggie boots. Heat rises from the ground, so if you can't walk barefoot on the streets, neither can your dog. If your dog's foot pads feel warm to the touch, cool them down with some water and stay off the hot pavement. You can find dog boots at your local pet store.

Many people don't have air-conditioning. With extreme temperatures this summer you will have to watch for signs of heatstroke indoors, also. To keep your furry friend from overheating indoors, try a cooling body wrap vest or mat, such as Keep Cool Mat. You can also give Rover doggie popsicles using peanut butter, berries or watermelon.

# Is your pet overweight?

You just got home after taking your pooch for his yearly booster at the veterinarian. You never expected to hear that he was overweight. What's a couple of pounds when he seems happy and healthy enough?

According to the Association for Pet Obesity Prevention's (APOP) latest veterinary survey, 53 percent of adult dogs in the United States are classified as overweight or obese by their veterinarians. Being obese can shorten your pet's lifespan.

The bigger problem, according to APOP founder Dr. Ernie Ward, is that pet owners don't even realize their chubby four-legged friends have a weight problem.

You may think that your pudgy pug or extra-large and lovable Labrador is adorable, but the additional pounds he's carrying can cause medical conditions and physical limitations that in the long run shorten your time together.

Many of the medical and physical conditions associated with overweight or obese humans are the same in pets. Just a few extra pounds on your furry friend can put them at risk for diabetes, heart and kidney disease, joint problems, high blood pressure and cancer.

Without a scale it's hard to know if your dog is overweight. Veterinarians use a rating system called the body condition score to determine whether a pet is in the "danger zone." Most pet parents have no idea that the ideal weight for their pet is not a number, but a certain ratio. You want ribs to be easily felt, but not necessarily seen, and a defined waist.

You should never start your pet on a diet without the assistance of your veterinarian. There may be a medical condition that could be causing Rover's excess weight.

As a pet parent, it can be difficult to determine just how much food you should be giving him. For that reason, regular veterinary exams should include an evaluation of your pet's body condition; your veterinarian can help you determine whether Rover has a weight issue and can help you decide on a proper diet and safe quantity to feed your pet daily.

If your dog is overweight your vet may have you regulate the amount of food you give your pet. Exercise is also important in maintaining your pet's weight or helping your pet to lose weight. However, if Rover is not used to strenuous exercise, start slowly. Gradually increase the pace and duration as he becomes more fit.

Get in the habit of daily walks; it's a great form of exercise for dogs. Regular exercise will not only help burn excess calories for your dog but will also provide mental stimulation and keep joints and muscles flexible and healthy.

You can make mealtime more fun with interactive feeding toys. These not only stimulate your pet's mind, they make him work for his supper;

and when pets eat more slowly they use up more calories. You may not necessarily need to change your dogs food; it's the amount of food that's the problem. Avoid table scraps and make sure you account for treats when deciding how much to feed your dog during meals.

Keeping your fury family member's weight in check is easier when you check it regularly. Your dog should typically lose about a pound per month, and monthly weigh-ins at the veterinarian's office will help you determine whether or not your dog's weight-loss program is working. Remember that working with your veterinarian in determining this plan and making sure it's working will guide you and your pet back on track to a healthy weight.

# Healthy "people food" for your dog

So Rover has finally learned to sit quietly and not beg at the table during dinnertime. What an accomplishment for your furry friend. But now that he's been so good, doesn't he deserve a table scrap?

When most pet parents are thinking of "people food" or table scraps, they're thinking of leftover hunks of fat, pizza crust, bones, or chunks of gravy on mashed potatoes. These types of table scraps are NOT healthy for your dog. Those types of scraps are usually very high in fat and calories and low in nutrients, plus these rich tidbits may also cause digestive upset and can contribute to pancreatitis, and could pose a choking hazard for your dog. Another common concern with feeding table scraps is that it causes obesity, while this is certainly a concern, it doesn't need to be the case.

So, while most people have heard that sharing food directly from your plate isn't the best idea, there are lots of table scraps that are safe and healthy to share with your pooch. Many pet parents make their own dog food, and their dogs eat "people foods" without a problem. If you look at the can or bag you feed your dog every day, and look at the ingredients, you can see that it's food that we eat also, such as chicken, sweet potatoes, peas and maybe a few grains.

Remember, dogs are omnivores like us and can eat a healthy variety, too. Some of the foods to avoid for your furry family member are high-fat foods like bacon, sausage, gravy-covered meat, beef trimmings and poultry skin.

Several common seasonings, including onions, garlic and chives can create problems for your furry friend by triggering irritation in their gastrointestinal tract, possibly leading to serious red-blood-cell damage, and even liver damage.

Avocados are also toxic to dogs and contain an element known as persin in their leaves, fruit, seeds, and even bark.

Caffeine is harmful to animals due to the presence of methylxanthines, chemicals which can be found not just in coffee, but also tea, colas, energy drinks and chocolate. But chocolate is a double whammy of sorts to your furry friend because it also contains theobromine, another potentially toxic element that can trigger reactions like vomiting and spasms.

And remember, though grapes and raisins offer nutritional benefits for humans, it's imperative to keep them out of your dogs reach. Macadamia nuts might make a great souvenir from a Hawaiian vacation, but it's a treat that can prove fatal for your pooch, whether eaten raw or roasted. If you have a weak spot for macadamia nuts, make sure to keep the jar tightly closed and out of your dog's reach at all times.

Knowing what your dog cannot indulge in makes life easier for both of you.

So what people food is healthy and nutritional to share with Rover?

When you think healthy for yourself, you are thinking healthy for your dog. Fresh fruits, veggies and lean meats are the best treats for your pooch.

Many veterinarians recommend that pet parents do not share table scraps with their pets; if you do plan to share with your dog, the following foods are pet-friendly and low in fat and sugar:

You can serve your pet fresh fruits and veggies such as slices of pears, cantaloupe, oranges, bananas, blackberries, green beans and seedless watermelon. And don't forget to pack a baggie for that car trip with summer around the corner with small slices of carrots, apples, strawberries and blueberries, it can help hydrate your furry friend.

Note that although you can give your dog apple slices, do not give him the core or the seeds, which contain arsenic.

Adding a teaspoon of canned pumpkin or sweet potatoes once in a while to Rover's dinner is a great treat. Both are a good source of fiber and beta carotene.

Always check with your veterinarian when introducing any new food.

Lean meat is also an excellent treat for your four-legged friend. Lean chicken, turkey, fish (make sure it's cooked well, raw salmon carries a parasite that can make dogs sick), or beef are great sources of protein. Even adding eggs to your dog's breakfast is a healthy treat. But make sure to use cooked egg because raw egg whites can cause biotin deficiency.

The key to healthy table scraps is moderation. Let your vet know what you are sharing with your pooch. And to maintain your dog's weight, keep those healthy table scraps to a minimum, especially for tiny dogs.

# What *should* you feed your dog?

Dogs have had 15,000 years to evolve from being primarily meat-eaters into omnivores capable of digesting both animal and plant nutrients. When it comes to nutrition, dogs are a lot like people. They can live healthy lives while eating a variety of food. Meats, vegetables, and grains, all can be a part of your dog's diet.

If you want to get technical, dogs actually belong to a category of meat-eaters called "facultative carnivores," which is so close in functional behavior to the omnivore category that it is hardly distinguishable.

People are very passionate when it comes to the subject of what they feed their dogs, and with good reason. A good, nutritional diet can contribute to a long and healthy life and psychological well-being for our furry friends. So what is the best food to feed domesticated dogs?

It is hard to sort out the truth from marketing.

Grain-free dog foods are currently very popular. But are they really healthier for your dog than other types of dog foods? A grain-free or meat-based dog food naturally contains fewer carbohydrates than grain-based foods. Some grain-free dog foods replace the grain with other types of starch like potato, sweet potato, tapioca, or green peas. The benefit of a grain-free dog food is that they mimic a dog's natural ancestral diet, and they tend to be considered hypo-allergenic, which is good for dogs that have food allergies.

The most common grains are wheat, rice, oats, corn, barley, millet, oatmeal, and quinoa. All grains are a good source of carbohydrates, which provide the body with energy. Some pets do better on diets with quality grains because of their high fiber content. Fiber in the diet is good for the overall gastrointestinal health of your pooch and may help some dogs keep their weight down. However, too much fiber in your pooch's diet can interfere with the digestion of other important nutrients in the food and result in loose stools.

Recognize that each dog is different, just like humans.

It comes down to one important concept; nutritionally, the most important aspect of a dog food is whether the food provides complete and balanced nutrition for your furry friend. And this is true regardless of whether the food contains grains or not.

Deciding between wet and dry food for your pooch can also be tough. Dry kibble is easier to store and serve. Wet often contains fewer grains and more protein.

Wet food is roughly 70 to 80 percent water and contains more protein, which can be beneficial for some dogs. Since it also contains more moisture, it is good for hydration and the urinary tract, and many dogs find it more palatable.

Dry food is only about 10 percent water and is easy to store and measure out. It benefits your dog's teeth and gums, helps ensure firm stools and is lower in cost per serving.

If you have a dog with special issues, it is best to consult your veterinarian for food recommendations. Dogs, like people, react differently to different diets. Some need mostly protein, some need lots of carbohydrates, so some benefit most from dry kibble and some from canned food.

Whether dry or canned, check the label to make sure that it is a nutritious diet for Rover. In some ways, the labels on the food you eat and the food your dog eats aren't so different.

One thing to look for is the Association of American Feed Control Official (AAFCO) seal of approval that will tell you that the food is nutritionally complete and balanced.

To really choose the best food takes some research or requires finding someone knowledgeable who you trust to advise what is right for your dog. Typically your vet or a trained nutritionist is the best resource to help you make decisions for your dog.

# Pets play pivotal role for older adults

You and your dog just got back from visiting a friend, an older adult who lives alone. Every week you've been over to visit her with Rover, and it seems to light up her life. She really perks up and smiles when she pets him. In fact your friend is deciding to adopt an older dog for herself.

Researchers are now finding that the most serious disease for older adults is not cancer or heart disease: It's loneliness. Loneliness can become an unwelcome companion as we get older, and can lead to depression as well as physical problems. Older adults who recently lost a spouse or who had other significant changes in their life are more likely to become lonely or depressed.

It's only recently that studies have begun to scientifically explore the benefits of the human-animal bond. The American Heart Association has linked having pets, especially dogs, with a reduced risk for heart disease and greater longevity. Researchers have also found that interacting with pets lowers blood pressure and pulse rate.

Studies show that the health of older adults who suffer from depression decline rapidly compared to seniors who are active, always around other people or with pets at home. Pets also provide a feeling of safety for those living alone, and decrease feelings of isolation. Pets can help older adults by supplying companionship and affection. Playing with a pet can elevate levels of serotonin and dopamine, which calm and relax.

Older adults with pets in the home are more likely to meet people and start new friendships. Pets keep older adults more active in the community. Pet parents have common interests and activities that provide the opportunity to build social bonds with new individuals. They may even gain a new interest in having their furry friend become a therapy visitor to assisted livings or other health facilities or schools.

Pets provide routine and a sense of responsibility. Having a pet that requires regular outdoor activity helps seniors stay connected to life. The daily walk out in the fresh air with their furry friend can keep them healthier longer, and linked to the community.

Older adults also keep active by feeding, grooming and caring for their pets. A study published in the Journal of the American Geriatrics Society demonstrated that independently living older adults who had pets tended to have better physical health and mental wellbeing than those that did not. They were more active, coped better with stress, and had better overall health than their contemporaries without pets.

Pets benefit, too, particularly when older folks adopt older pets. An older dog is harder to adopt out of a shelter than younger dogs or puppies. So when a senior adopts an older dog, it gets to go from pound to paradise. Since older adults are retired, they have lots of time to devote to a previously unwanted pet.

Because people age so differently, the decision to become a pet parent needs to be made carefully. If you don't like change or have physical limitations, you may not be a good candidate. You'll benefit most from having a pet whose needs are compatible with your lifestyle and physical capabilities.

Pet parenting may not be the right answer for some older folks. Luckily, it isn't always necessary for someone to take on the full responsibility of pet parenting to reap the physical and emotional benefits of interacting with a four-legged companion. If you're not able to handle the demands of having a pet, you can still ask to walk a neighbor's dog, or volunteer at an animal shelter. A visit from a therapy dog could work wonders for someone who has physical limitations.

Using pets to offset emotional and physical problems and to improve quality of life is especially beneficial to seniors. It takes just a bit of careful planning to find the right mixture, whether it's becoming a pet parent or helping out at a shelter. Most animal shelters or rescue groups welcome volunteers to help care for homeless pets or assist at adoption events. Even short periods of time spent with a pet can benefit you and the animal.

# Picking up after Rover

You're out walking Rover on a beautiful spring day with your usual doggie waste baggies tucked in your back pocket. You head out to the park and just when you and Rover are walking through the freshly cut grass, you almost slip after stepping in a big pile of dog poop, left by some less-considerate pet parent.

It's not just a huge annoyance, but an actual health hazard! Cities and neighborhoods know about this problem and keep a supply of dog waste baggies near the parks for anyone to use all year round. Yet the problem still remains.

Cleaning up after your furry friend can be a stinky job, but someone's got to do it. Cleaning up is necessary for a healthy environment for you and your family.

Remember when you first received your adorable furry friend and actively agreed to provide him with love, food, and shelter? Sanitation and cleanup are also important facets of being a responsible pet parent.

Picking up after your pooch, is high on the list of dog walking etiquette, along with walking Rover on a leash and keeping him under control during walks.

There are reasons why you should clean up after your dog.

Cleaning up after Rover, shows respect for your neighbors and the community. Some people think its okay to leave dog waste because it will break down naturally. However, the biodegrading process is very slow, and, especially in places where the dog population is high, dog waste can accumulate faster than it breaks down. Dog waste is not fertilizer.

Did you know that dog poop is a major contributor to stormwater pollution?

Scientists have discovered that dog waste is a major cause of water pollution and therefore poses a hazard to human health. Rain and melting snow flows across yards, dog parks, down trails, etc. on its way to creeks via the streets and storm drains. Dog poop contains bacteria and is high in nitrogen and phosphorus (nutrients that negatively affect the water)

Dog waste also contains disease transmitting organisms such as roundworms, and bacteria such as E. coli, and in sufficiently high amounts these bacteria can make people sick. Intestinal bacteria commonly found in dogs and cats (regardless of the type of food they are consuming) include E. coli, salmonella, clostridia and campylobacter. These bugs don't cause problems in healthy pets, but they can cause intestinal disease in humans. The bacteria are present in your pet's poop.

However, most human infections from these bacteria are the result of someone coming in contact with pet feces on their hands, and then touching their mouth or face. Children who play on the ground outside are particularly at risk!

The quickest way to get rid of your furry friends waste is to put it in a plastic bag, which you can usually find at parks in dispensers. Then just drop the bag in a trash can.

You can make a difference by being a responsible pet parent. Be prepared. Carry bags with you to pick up pet waste. And it's a good idea to carry a few extras with you in case you meet someone in need. Please do not leave bags on the side of trails, there isn't anyone designated to pick them up!

By routinely picking up after your pet, you are part of the solution! And your actions will help convey the message that it's the right thing to do.

# How to deal with dogs who bite

The cutest little dog wagged his tail when you approached him at the park. How could it have turned into an aggressive dog and bite you when all you did was put out your hand for him to sniff?

Be aware of the fact that any dog can bite, from the smallest to the largest. Never approach an unfamiliar dog, respect his space and teach your children to do the same.

National Dog Bite Prevention Week is May 18-24. This week is the time to raise awareness of canine behavior through education, as well as encouraging responsible pet-parenting. Educating folks about how to interact properly with any dog is critically important when it comes to reducing dog-bite incidents.

Approximately 4.5 million people are bitten by dogs in the United States every year, and one fifth of them end up needing medical attention for their wounds. Children are, by far, the most common victims of dog bites and are more likely to be severely injured.

According to State Farm Insurance, Oregon ranks 13 on the top 15 states for dog-bite claims.

Dogs are members of the family; so many owners think that their furry friend won't bite. Any dog can bite, regardless of the breed.

Start with your own four-legged friend. There is no way to guarantee that your dog will never bite someone. But you can significantly reduce the risk.

First it is important to spay or neuter your dog. This important routine procedure will reduce your dog's desire to roam and fight with other dogs. Spayed or neutered dogs are much less likely to bite.

Socialize your dog as soon as possible by introducing him to many different types of people and situations so that he isn't nervous or frightened under normal social circumstances. Enrolling your dog in a training class is an excellent way to socialize him and to learn proper training techniques. Since training Rover is a family matter, every member of the household should participate in his instruction techniques. Dogs that are well-trained and socialized are much less likely to bite.

Exercise and play with your furry friend on a regular basis to reinforce the human-animal bond. An exercised dog will less likely have pent-up nervous energy that can lead to biting. For everyone's safety, don't let your dog roam unleashed.

Set appropriate limits for your dog's behavior. Don't wait for an accident. The first time he shows signs of dangerous behavior toward any person, seek professional help from your veterinarian, an animal behaviorist, or a qualified dog trainer.

Be a responsible pet parent by licensing your dog as required by law and providing regular veterinary care, including rabies vaccinations.

So now that Rover is well trained and under your supervision at all times, you can breathe a little easier. But what about dogs outside of the home that you or your child might come in contact with?

Knowing the common triggers that cause dog bites will empower you to avoid these situations. Dog bites are always preceded by behavior that a keen observer can use as a warning and then take steps to reduce the dog's stress or fear. The dogs ears are typically pinned back, the fur along their back may stand up, and you may be able to see the whites of their eyes. Non-social "stand-offish" behavior such as freezing in response to a touch or look followed by direct eye contact back from the dog is another clear sign that he may bite.

Children should not approach, touch or play with any dog that's sleeping, eating, chewing on a toy or bone, or caring for puppies. Dogs are more likely to bite if they're startled, frightened, or caring for young. Take the time to educate your children on how to act around dogs, what to watch for, and what to do if a dog attacks.

Never leave a baby or small child alone with a dog, even if it's your family pet. Children are often bitten by a dog in their own household. Teach your child to ask permission before touching or playing with any dog.

If a child sees a dog off-leash outside, she should not approach the dog and should tell an adult immediately.

Remember, dog-bite prevention begins at home, with your own dog, by being a responsible pet parent.

# When your dog can't travel with you

This holiday season, you've been invited to your granddaughter's home two states away. You haven't seen her in three years, so you decide to take the family on the road for a visit. You'd love to take your four-legged family member too, except for one major problem: Rover gets motion sickness and vomits in the car on trips more than 10 minutes away.

Even though many people prefer to take their pets along, it's not always possible for numerous reasons. What options do you have in leaving your precious pooch behind?

The best way to ensure that your time away is fun and stress-free for both you and your dog is to have a good game plan in advance of departure. Though dogs have different personalities, maintaining a sense of normalcy and routine during your absence is beneficial for every type of dog.

When it comes to the care that your dog will receive when you are away, the best-case scenario is probably one in which the dog remains at home with a trusted friend or family member. Being able to stay in the home with familiar surroundings could be the best situation for your pooch. However, every dog is different and not everyone has close friends or family members nearby ready to help. There are other options.

If your dog is the type that needs to stay in his own home while you're away or if you worry about your dog travelling to a kennel or being in unfamiliar surroundings, then it's time that you have an established network of trusted, responsible pet-sitters that can make your absence much easier on your dog. To determine the best pet-sitter for your furry friend, you could interview various candidates. This way, you can introduce them to Rover, and see if they interact well.

Some pet-sitters will take care of your dog in their own home. Be sure that any sitter who cares for your pet in their house is ready to take on the responsibility of your pet's needs. Check references before hiring a sitter and it's a good idea to let your pet visit the home before your scheduled time away. Since dogs have incredible scent memories, it would be helpful to leave Rover's bed and familiar toys with the sitter. It will make him feel more at home.

Another option is a boarding kennel or doggie daycare. Boarding kennels offer a place where your dog can be looked after by professionals, without giving them access to your home. Dogs by nature are social animals. The more your dog interacts with other dogs the better their social skills become. Doggie daycare or boarding kennels usually offer the opportunity for your dog to be paired with one or several dogs for playtime and to learn socialization skills while getting rid of excess energy.

It is important to do some research before leaving your dog at a daycare or kennel. Try to visit before you leave your dog there. You can tour the facility to make sure it is clean and has enough room for your dog to exercise.

Whether your pooch is staying at your home, the sitter's house or a boarding kennel, making a list of detailed instructions is very important. Remember to make sure his vaccinations are up-to-date, and his identification tag is on his collar. Leave the sitter a list of numbers: the vet, a friend's number and yours.

Parting with your dog can be tough, but having a system to keep Rover happy and healthy in your absence will make your travels much easier. Plan ahead and look forward to a fun reunion when you return.

Oh, and be sure to bring home treats!

# The Hidden Dangers of Summertime

You've been playing ball outdoors with Rover for over 20 minutes on a very warm sunny day; suddenly he begins to pant heavily and starts to vomit. You had forgotten how hot it was outside, since you were wearing shorts and sandals. Lucky for you that Rover began to cool down once you brought him inside the house in the air-conditioning and began to get hydrated again with a big bowl of water.

Summer can be a very dangerous time for your pets. Most people remember about things like fleas and ticks. However, the biggest danger to your furry friend during the summer is something you can't see, smell or hear. Heat stroke is a common occurrence in dogs. Most people won't recognize the early warning signs that a dog is suffering from heat exhaustion, which left untreated leads to heat stroke and ultimately death.

Dehydration can happen as a result of overheating. Be sure your dog has access to plenty of water, whether you are out playing with him or he is left alone when you are running errands, since it's too hot to take him in the car with you.

If you're hot, your furry friend is even hotter. Providing shade, shelter and fresh water to your dog when he is outside is extremely important during the summer.

Always supervise your dog. No matter where he is, or how well you might think he is trained, you need to keep an eye on your pooch. There are too many unknown hazards that could hurt him, whether playing ball in a park or just clowning around by the river.

Make sure you bring Rover's leash and collar, even if he won't be restrained while playing.

You and your furry pal may want to cool down at the Coast to have fun in the sun and water, but did you know that dehydration can occur when your pooch is right next to the water? Salt water can be harmful to animals. Ingesting the salt increases dehydration, because it draws water into the intestines. Salt water can also cause vomiting and diarrhea, and lead to bigger problems, if your dog doesn't get clean fresh water.

Dogs, just like humans, can also get sunburn, which can lead to skin cancer. If Rover has light-colored fur on the nose or ears, they are more susceptible to skin cancer. Keep him inside if possible during the hottest part of the day.

Freshwater lakes and rivers are abundant in Oregon and loads of fun for everyone, including your furry pal. Many pet parents remove their dog's collar and tags while playing in the water or on a boat. If lost, your furry friend may not be able to return home

Get a pet life-jacket for your dog, and train him to wear it while boating. Like humans, even the strongest swimmer can get a leg cramp.

While some freshwater algae may be harmless, freshwater lakes still provide their own set of hazards, and one of the most dangerous is toxic algae levels and parasites. It is much safer to bring along your own fresh cool water for your dog to drink.

Summertime can be perfect for backyard barbecues, parties and going to festivals, but remember that the food and drink being served may be poisonous to your dog.

Backyard barbecues can be fun, but sometimes Rover can be quicker than you think and grab a piece of meat, like a chicken leg off the table in no time. It doesn't matter whether they're from chicken wings or pork ribs, cooked meat bones cause all sorts of problems, especially if they get lodged in the mouth or throat. Make sure your guests have somewhere to dispose of their carnivorous waste well out of your pooch's way.

It might be best to leave Rover at home when going to large outdoor festivals or events. A crowd can be overwhelming and it increases the chances of injury, dehydration and exhaustion. Loud noises could cause him to frighten and suddenly pull away from you, even while on a leash.

The bottom line: keep an eye on your dog and don't leave him unattended. It's important to exercise common sense and proceed with caution to help keep your dog safe, like any other member of the family. Summertime comes with its own set of hazards, so make sure you are familiar with the risks. Learn what warning signs mean trouble and when in doubt, call your veterinarian right way. The summer will be much easier for you and your dog to enjoy!

# The pros and cons of pet rescue

Pets share our homes, keep us company, and can reduce feelings of stress. They offer us companionship, go along with us on walks, and greet us at the end of each workday. They give us unconditional love.

So it's understandable that sooner or later you might desire to add an adopted furry friend to your home.

But remember that adopting a pet is a serious commitment. What kind of pet will be the best fit for your household? Consider how much time you'd need to devote to the daily needs of your new animal friend such as walking, grooming and playtime. What available space do you have? A small dog or a cat could be right for an apartment. A large dog might need a fenced yard.

Doing your homework in advance will make your search easier and increase the chances that your new pet will be a happy addition to the family.

Deciding to adopt an animal from a shelter or private rescue agency can be a huge decision on many different levels. Reviewing some of the pros and cons may help you make that critical decision.

Shelters large and small always have a good selection of animals looking for new homes. According to The Humane Society of the United States, 6 to 8 million pets end up in shelters each year and only about half of those will be adopted. You can find a variety of ages from kittens and puppies to senior pets that fit your lifestyle.

Unfortunately, almost half of the dogs and cats submitted to local humane societies in the U.S. are euthanized (about 3 to 4 million annually). By adopting a pet from a shelter or rescue group you are giving that animal a second chance at a new healthy life and happy home.

There are many reasons dogs and cats end up in shelters or rescue organizations: death of a guardian, new baby, change in work schedule, owners who develop financial difficulties or move to a place where pets are not allowed, etc. Some dogs and cats may be strays found out and about or may be brought in from other shelters.

Since animals adopted from shelters and rescue groups have had their first set of shots and have been spayed or neutered, they typically cost less than pets purchased or even acquired for free. Once you add in the cost of the vaccinations, spay/neuter surgery, microchip, dewormer, and other extras, you'll be surprised what a bargain an adopted pet really is!

One of the great benefits of adopting a dog older than six months or so from a shelter is that usually they are housebroken. But if you decide you want a young puppy, there are plenty to choose from.

Even if you're smitten with the idea of sharing your home with a specific purebred dog, chances are that there's a breed rescue group or shelter in your vicinity with just the right pup in need of a family.

One of the cons of adopting from shelters is that you may not be able to find the right breed or size of the dog that you want right away. But don't be discouraged; sadly, shelters and rescue groups receive new animals every day, so keep checking back with them. Some groups keep a waiting list, so they can call you if an animal matches your preferences becomes available.

Another possible downside is behavioral issues with your new pet. Your new furry friend you've just adopted from the local humane society may turn out different than you expected. The act of being surrendered to a shelter or rescue is a traumatic experience on its own for a dog or cat, not to mention that you don't know what happened to them before they arrived there. Try to learn as much as possible about the animal you have chosen from the organization. They may be able to provide you a lot more information about the animal's background than you might think.

A last thought on rescue pets: They seem eager to please. Maybe they knew that without you, their days were numbered. Maybe being alone for a period of their life made them appreciate a family more. Whatever the reason, a rescue can fill your life with happiness.

# Adding a Second Dog to Your Home

Thinking about adding an extra playmate for your pooch? Whether it's a companion for yourself, someone else in the family or your four legged friend, there are many things to consider.

When you are going to introduce a second dog to your home, think about your present dog first. Remember there are no set rules about good pooch matches because all dogs – even within the same breed – are individuals. Know your dog's personality and be realistic about the impact a second dog can have on him.

When done correctly, multiple dog homes can provide additional company, playtime and just plain fun for the current dog, not to mention you.

Before settling on a breed, think about the gender of the dog. As a generalization, a dog will tend to get along better with a dog of the opposite sex. Two females are more likely to fight than two males. If you're introducing a new dog of the same sex, you may want to consider spaying or neutering the new dog before the introduction.

Compatibility between your current pooch and the one in question comes down to several factors. What is the age and size difference? Play style and energy level?

You don't want a size difference so great that one dog could accidently injure the other. Age plays another factor. You wouldn't want to bring a rambunctious 7 month old German shepherd into a home with a 14 year old Chihuahua with painful arthritis, so think about spacing them just a few years apart. Finding a dog with a similar play style can ensure that the dogs don't feel threatened or overwhelmed by each other's behavior. It is very common for dogs to feed off each other's energy and actions.

You've finally spotted a potential match for your pooch on petfinder.com, a local shelter, or in foster care, etc., and it's time for introductions.

Ideally you will have the opportunity to introduce the two dogs before you make the commitment of adding the new dog to your home. Dogs are much less likely to behave in a dominant or aggressive manner if they first meet on neutral territory. If it's obtainable, have the dogs meet initially at a local dog park or a fenced in friend's yard. If you decided on adopting a dog at a shelter, take your pooch with you for the introductions there.

If possible have one person take both dogs for a walk, keeping them a short distance apart so they can get use to each other's presence. If all goes smoothly and they seem comfortable with each other, let them meet in a fenced area so they can interact with each other off leash.

When the two dogs are playing in a friendly manner, speak soothingly and positively to them to reinforce their positive interaction.

Sometimes introductions don't always go well the first time around, so you may try it again to see if repeated exposure to each other helps the dogs calm down and get more used to each other.

One thing to remember, when a new dog is introduced into the household, attention can sometimes be directed towards the new family member making your old dog feel left out. Give your original pooch the same amount of attention and time that he received prior to the new dog being introduced.

Good Luck! Life is never boring with two dogs.

# Separation anxiety in dogs

You had a change in routine with a new job, and your furry friend isn't handling it well. When Rover hears you pick up your keys to go, he starts whining, gets restless and runs to the door hoping he can go too. Then when you return home later, he's wild with joy and follows you around. But you also find a couple of your slippers chewed up in little pieces, and you also notice scratch marks on the front door. Rover had been scratching and digging to get out for the few hours that you've been gone.

One of the most common complaints of pet parents is that their dog is disruptive or destructive when left alone. Their pooch might urinate, defecate (even though he is house trained), bark, howl, chew, dig or try to escape. These can all be symptoms of distress.

You may be dealing with a case of separation anxiety.

The term gets tossed around and talked about casually, but separation anxiety is a serious matter. True separation anxiety is your dog's panicked response to being left alone.

Separation anxiety is triggered when dogs become upset because of separation from their human companions. And each dog handles it differently. Some dogs suffering from separation anxiety become agitated when their pet parent leaves. Others seem anxious or depressed.

Separation anxiety ranges anywhere from mild to extreme. An example of extreme separation anxiety could be a dog that will attempt to dig and chew through doors or windows, which could result in self-injury, such as broken teeth, cut and scraped front paws and damaged nails.

Separation anxiety can occur in animals from multiple or single-pet homes. It may be more likely to occur in animals with a history of abuse. Or dogs that have had a traumatic separation from a previous owner, such as a dog brought into a shelter may have an increased risk. Dogs that have missed out on normal social interaction with people or other animals, especially as puppies, may also be at risk.

A dog that has never had a prior problem may develop separation anxiety when there is a change in the routine, such as when a pet parent's work schedule is altered or when the family moves into a new home. Some dogs may just develop the disorder as they grow older, and some breeds seem to be genetically susceptible.

Remember - your furry friend's behavior is a part of a panic response. Your dog isn't trying to punish you! He just wants you to come home. Scolding or punishing Rover may only lead to confusion, more anxiety, and worse behavior.

If you feel your dog has separation anxiety, the first step is to discuss the situation with your veterinarian immediately. It's important to make sure that Rover's behavior is really due to separation anxiety and not a medical issue.

Separation anxiety is preventable if you're starting with a puppy. Unfortunately, sometimes separation anxiety just isn't preventable, especially with an older dog. But thanks to desensitization, crating techniques, and an understanding of the disorder, it's treatable.

Here are some effective techniques to help your furry friend with mild separation anxiety:

Some behaviorists suggest independence training in various forms - for instance, having your dog practice staying at a distance. Practice having your dog stay while you leave the room and come back. This training will help Rover learn that he can remain calm and happy in one place while you go to another room.

Take Rover for a brisk walk right before you leave the house. This might help him relax and rest while you're gone.

Counterconditioning might also reduce or resolve a mild case of separation anxiety. According to the ASPCA, counterconditioning is a treatment process that changes an animal's fearful, anxious or aggressive reaction to a pleasant, relaxed one instead.

It's done by associating the presence of a feared or disliked situation with something really good, something your dog loves. In other words, counterconditioning focuses on developing an association between being alone and good things or rewards, like delicious food. Your dog can learn that what he fears actually predicts good things for him.

Leave a food toy like a Kong stuffed with peanut butter or cottage cheese ready for him to dig into as soon as you leave. A Kong can be frozen so it takes more of Rover's time to focus on the delicious treat. This also eliminates boredom. Be sure to remove the special food toys as soon as you return home so that Rover only has access to them when you are gone. He might end up looking forward to you leaving after he's used to the routine.

Another technique is crate training. It can be helpful for some dogs. If they learn that the crate is their safe place to go when left alone. However, for other dogs, the crate can cause added stress and anxiety.

Separation anxiety has little to do with training or discipline; your dog's behaviors are a result of the severe panic your dog feels when you're not there. Left untreated, it causes damage to your house and belongings - and serious psychological suffering for your dog. Let your veterinarian know about your furry friend's behaviors. If you need more assistance resolving your furry friend's anxiety issues, consult a professional animal-behavior specialist.

# Chapter 46

# High-tech harness lets you communicate with your dog

If you're a dog parent, you may spend a lot of time wondering what you're dog is actually thinking about. Imagine being able to really know what your furry friend is thinking!

The relationship between humans and dogs is unlike any other. In fact, we sometimes forget that our furry family members that share our lives, homes and often our beds with us are a totally different species from our own.

However, according to Stanley Coren, a behaviorist from the University of British Columbia, dogs have the same brain structures that produce emotions in humans. They have the same hormones and undergo the same chemical changes that humans do in emotional states. Dogs even have the hormone ocytocin, which in humans is involved with love and affection.

People have long dreamt of being able to talk with their furry best friends, and now scientists at North Carolina State University have come up with a new device that will allow humans to communicate with dogs in a new unique way.

N.C. State researchers have developed a number of technologies that can be used to enhance communication between dogs and humans, which have applications for everything from search and rescue to service dogs to training your pets.

Researchers and developer Dr. David Roberts, a professor at N.C. State, has created a high-tech dog harness that fits comfortably onto a dog, and is equipped with a variety of technologies that they say allows dogs and humans to communicate using a computer.

According to Popular Science magazine, Roberts said, "We're at the dawn of a new era here, where technology is going to connect us to our pets in ways we haven't seen before." Roberts is also the co-lead author of a paper written about the invention.

Roberts also said, "It's a communication platform that is designed specifically to provide two-way remote computer-mediated communication between handlers and their dogs."

The prototype harness, called the Cyber-Enhanced Working Dog, has sensors that collect and interpret dogs' behavioral signals, and humans are able to send them appropriate commands.

The small computer on the harness, called BeagleBone Black, monitors the dog's movement, emotional state, and outside environment. Information is wirelessly transmitted back to the handler, who can interpret it from a distance.

The sensors read the dog's heart rate and body temperature to determine his emotional state, such as if the dog is stressed.

And according to Roberts, they can start to characterize things like stress, distraction, or excitement and help handlers become more aware of what their dogs are doing and why.

Human commands are translated for the dog through speakers and vibrating motors on the harness. Roberts says dogs would be trained to respond to almost 100 different signals in the same way they respond to voice and hand commands.

One goal of the device is to help handlers identify and alleviate stress for the dogs, improving the length and quality of a dog's life. For instance, dogs often communicate non-verbally, and handlers of guide dogs, of course, can't see non-verbal communication.

"We have a fully functional prototype, but we'll be redefining the design as we explore more and more application for the platform," Roberts said.

Shortly after developing the harness, the North Carolina State researchers teamed up with the Smart Emergency Response System project, which aims to integrate high-tech systems with search-and-rescue efforts.

"You're never going to replace the human element of search and rescue," Roberts said. "What we're really trying to do is help these dogs be safer and more efficient in doing their jobs."

And, according to Roberts, these types of technologies that they've been working on will be commercially available in the not-too-distant future.

This sort of communication device could also be used to treat dogs with separation anxiety, to calm anxious puppies at shelters, and to help guide dogs enhance the everyday lives of their pet parents.

# What's up with weird dog behaviors?

The sight of your dog whirling around in a circle trying to catch his tail in his mouth might be one of the funniest things you've ever seen. Could it be that your pooch just noticed he has a tail?

Though dogs are our best friends, they can sometimes be, well, a bit weird. You'd think after a lasting partnership of 20,000 years or so, that we'd have them figured out by now. Quirky dog behaviors may seem unusual to us, but for the most part are actually completely normal for them.

Instinct is a powerful force in the animal world. It brings about the behaviors necessary for survival. These instinctive or innate behaviors pass from generation to generation through the genes.

Tail-chasing is a behavior that often starts early on; a puppy becoming aware of his own individuality sees the tail and begins to whirl around after it. It serves his deep-seated instinctive need to chase something. Of course when his pet parents see this, they laugh and often encourage their pooch for more. And so the behavior slowly becomes ingrained.

Howling may not be music to your ears, but researchers believe that dog howling is a throwback to wolf heritage and that howls also have a variety of meanings. Have you ever noticed when a fire truck goes screeching by with its sirens blaring, that suddenly all the dogs in the neighborhood start howling?

In our civilized world many things sound a lot like howling. Fire sirens are one of them. So it could be that when some dogs hear this sound, they mimic the siren and start howling. Dogs can howl out of boredom, loneliness or seeking communication with other dogs. In the wild, wolves howl in an attempt to reassemble the pack after individuals travel in different directions.

Does your pooch greet you by rolling on his back? By rolling over onto his back and exposing one of his vulnerable areas, your pooch is showing you that he trusts you and that he understands you are the boss. Even though dogs are domesticated, they still recognize the same kind of pecking order as a wolf pack might; rolling onto the back is a show of submission to the alpha of the pack. Rolling over also helps wolves get out of potential danger by peacefully persuading an aggressor to back off.

Some of our furry friends just like to sleep on their backs, which mean he's comfortable around you and he feels safe.

Have you ever watched your four-legged friend twirl around two or three times before settling into a sleeping spot? While this may seem like a wacky, meaningless act, it actually has some meaning behind it. The circling around is most probably an innate behavior for dogs because in the wild, they would circle around repeatedly, to trample down grass or weeds to dislodge any bits of uncomfortable debris before settling down for the night.

Your pooch hasn't seen you all day, and when you return home do you find a happy dog that can't seem to stop licking you? Right from birth that is how the mother communicates with her newborn pups, it's how she stimulates them to start breathing and how she cleans them when they are born, so it's very important to the survival of puppies.

In the wild and in domestic dogs, you'll find they will lick around the mother's mouth as pups and still retain that instinct. It is most probably a submissive gesture; the more subordinate members of a pack will lick the more dominant members, and that's important in maintaining pack harmony.

Did you know that licking also releases pleasurable endorphins which give dogs a feeling of comfort and pleasure? It can be a sign of affection and relieves stress.

Most folks have a dog that will sometimes exhibit a weird behavior, but remember before you attribute it as just another silly practice, there also may be medical reasons why Rover is acting a certain way.

One example of a weird behavior that needs medical attention may look funny and cause laughter, but scooting across the floor on his bottom may be done to relieve a painful anal sac.

It's just another day in the life of a dog; chasing his tail, licking his human's face and turning around a few times before taking a nap.

# Dog safety during the holidays

It's that time of year again, and along with the excitement and merriment of the holidays come possible dangers to your dog. And like many people, you probably consider your dog to be an important member of the family, so of course you want to include him in your holiday festivities.

So, before you deck the halls with boughs of holly, think twice if you have dogs in the household.

Holly is poisonous to pets. Bright ornamental plants are a great way to dress up the house during the holidays but keep holly, mistletoe, poinsettia, and any forms of lily out of your pet's reach.

There's nothing like a real Christmas tree during the holidays, the pine fragrance is so appealing. Your furry friends think so, too. Use caution:

Christmas trees are considered to be mildly toxic. The fir tree oils can be irritating to the mouth and stomach.

Puppies may want to jump up on your fresh-smelling tree; after all, you've brought the outdoors inside for them. Before decorating your holiday tree, try to secure it to the wall or ceiling so it doesn't tip and fall causing possible injury to your pet.

All the boxes of decorations are out and it's time to trim that beautiful Douglas fir Christmas tree. Don't put lights on the lower branches of your tree. The lights may get hot and possible burn your pet. The wires may entice your animal friends into chewing them and getting shocked. Keep electrical cords out of reach.

When decorating your Christmas tree, avoid glass ornaments, which break easily and may cut a dog or cat's feet or mouth. Children enjoy stringing cranberries and popcorn for an old-fashioned Christmas tree look, but remember edible ornaments can be dangerously tempting to your pets. They could end up knocking over the tree and everything on it in an attempt to reach those goodies. Keep other ornaments off the lower branches so your pet cannot get ahold of them.

Do not use tinsel, garland, or angel hair on your tree. These sparkly items are especially attractive to puppies, and when eaten can cause blockages which may require surgery to remove.

Although ribbons and string make your holiday packages look festive, they pose significant dangers to your pets. Like tinsel, these items can be ingested and cause intestinal obstruction.

It's tempting to give our four-legged friends a taste of what we like to eat around the holidays. Some of the things we eat and drink can cause serious illness in dogs.

Did you know that giving your pet a piece of holiday ham can lead to life-threatening pancreatitis? Be careful of what your furry friends eat during the holidays. Giving your dog bits of holiday cookies or pie can cause diarrhea from too much sugar. Remember, chocolate is poisonous for your furry friend. Keep alcoholic drinks out of reach. Sometimes at parties alcoholic beverages are spilled on the floor or left where your pet can reach them. Alcohol poisoning in pets is more common than you think.

The holidays are both a wonderful and stressful time, with the constant stream of visitors and parties. Your dog may not be able to appreciate or understand the strange people, noises, and festivities associated with holiday celebrations. Stick as closely as possible to your normal routine. Try not to vary with your dogs feeding, walking and playtime schedule.

# Benefits of dog agility training

Since your furry friend was such an active puppy you signed him up for obedience class and he passed with flying colors. But now that Rover is over a year old, he seems bored and restless even though you walk him every day and have lots of playtime together. What could be missing?

The fastest-growing trend in the dog world is agility training. You've probably seen or heard about dog agility with the tunnels, teeter- totters and jumps. During the Sisters Doggie Dash talent contest in August, contestants used dog agility training to display their furry friend's talent.

Dog agility is a fast-paced canine competitive sport that tests your dog's intelligence, athletic ability and obedience skills on an obstacle course, with you as his handler. You and your dog work as a team, and as his handler you will help him navigate the obstacles in the right order. Running through a course that involves passing over and through a variety of obstacles will challenge Rover's mind and body, and give you exercise as well.

The sport began in England in 1978 and has grown in popularity. The agility course mimics the hunt for prey that a dog would experience in the wild. His natural instincts involve climbing slopes, jumping over logs, weaving through thick brush and under bushes. Since the goal is to catch up with prey, time is of the essence and the faster a dog runs, the better his chances of ending up with a satisfying meal. In other words; agility training provides an outlet for your dog's natural instincts.

As pet parents with high-energy dogs know, a bored dog is a mischievous dog. Agility training gives your dog two very important jobs: learning and performing. By giving him something to do, you'll stimulate his drive, curiosity, and intelligence. It's a fun way to bond with your furry friend. Even if you don't want to compete, dog agility training is enjoyable and fulfilling.

Will your dog enjoy agility activities? There's only one way to find out.

Involving your dog in agility will also help to strengthen his muscles, improve coordination, keep him fit, and increase endurance. Helping your dog to pass through agility obstacles will help reinforce basic obedience commands, improve communication between you and your furry friend and ultimately help to improve your dog's behavior outside of the agility course.

You will see all shapes and sizes of dogs doing agility, and that is one of the great things about the sport; any healthy dog, no matter what his size from a Papillion to a German shepherd, can have fun while burning off excess energy.

Remember, agility may not be right for every dog, but if your furry friend is playful and energetic, he will probably enjoy it. Remember to have your veterinarian examine Rover for fitness before starting any exercise program. Dogs who are too young, to fat or too old, or who have medical conditions, such as heart problems or joint problems may not be good candidates for dog agility.

Your dog needs to be in top physical health before starting any training program, especially one as rigorous as agility.

Dogs usually start agility training around a year old, and because puppies may injure themselves by jumping hurdles, talk to your veterinarian to figure out when your pup would be ready to attempt the jumps and other obstacles on the course.

In order to be successful at agility training, your pooch should know basic obedience commands. Obedience training will also improve your dog's confidence and self-esteem: Dogs like knowing the rules and thrive when successfully completing a task, especially when there's a treat for them.

Begin basic obedience by teaching your dog to sit, come, heel, and stay. Your pooch will also benefit from attending group training classes. There he will learn basic obedience, and get used to working around lots of other dogs and people.

Once your dog is ready to start agility training, your best bet is to find a class or group in your area.

Though it may not be right for every dog, agility training offers a plethora of benefits, including mental and physical stimulation, opportunities for bonding, and increased confidence and drive. No matter how you score, agility is a win-win.

# When barking becomes a nuisance

How many times have you gone on a pleasant walk by yourself or with your pooch only to hear rowdy barking through a fence or from across the street and have it continue until you're out of earshot?

Barking is natural; it's how dogs communicate with each other and with you. Sometimes we want our dogs to bark in order to warn us of potential danger or that someone is on the property. However, continuous barking is annoying, for you and your neighbors.

Nuisance barking is a habit which is correctable in most pets with proper training.

Try to determine why your dog is barking. Excessive barking can be the result of boredom, stress, loneliness, and a need for attention. Understanding the reason why your dog barks is the first step toward controlling the behavior. Shouting at your dog to stop barking does not help. It may actually cause him to bark more.

Your dog needs to understand when to bark and when to be quiet, and it's your job to teach this to your pooch. You'll need to work on your dog's barking issue right away. The longer you wait, the harder it is to curb the problem. Plus, it's one of the fastest ways to turn neighbors into enemies and get a visit from the local sheriff.

There are numerous techniques that can help stop your dog from barking. While all of them can be very successful, you shouldn't expect miraculous results overnight.

Before you try any training techniques, make sure your dog is well-exercised. A dog may be barking out of sheer boredom or because of pent-up energy. Avoid leaving a dog alone for long periods of time.

There are many possible techniques that would be right for your particular pet. Here is an example of a common one: Determine your command phrase for correcting your pooch when he barks. This can be "No Bark" or "Quiet." Whatever you feel comfortable with is fine. When your dog barks, correct him each and every time by using your catch phrase and giving Rover a favorite treat immediately after he stops barking, even for only a second. You must be consistent and correct him each time, as you do not want your dog to get confused as to when he can and cannot bark.

After you give your dog a treat, praise your furry friend for being a good dog and being quiet. Do this each time he barks. Each time you do this with your pooch, wait a few seconds longer after your catch-phrase before giving a treat, holding the treat in front of him. Each time the dog barks, extend the time that he will wait for the treat, while being quiet. Everyone in your family needs to be included in the training, including a pet-sitter.

Whatever technique you use, remember your dog will not be trained overnight. It takes time to break the habit of excessive barking. Keep your training sessions positive and upbeat. Remain calm and patient, and eventually he will bark only when appropriate.

Consult your veterinarian and/or trainer if you continue to face barking issues despite your best efforts.

How many times have you gone on a pleasant walk by yourself or with your pooch only to hear rowdy barking through a fence or from across the street and have it continue until you're out of earshot?

Barking is natural; it's how dogs communicate with each other and with you. Sometimes we want our dogs to bark in order to warn us of potential danger or that someone is on the property. However, continuous barking is annoying, for you and your neighbors.

Nuisance barking is a habit which is correctable in most pets with proper training.

Try to determine why your dog is barking. Excessive barking can be the result of boredom, stress, loneliness, and a need for attention. Understanding the reason why your dog barks is the first step toward controlling the behavior. Shouting at your dog to stop barking does not help. It may actually cause him to bark more.

Your dog needs to understand when to bark and when to be quiet, and it's your job to teach this to your pooch. You'll need to work on your dog's barking issue right away. The longer you wait, the harder it is to curb the problem. Plus, it's one of the fastest ways to turn neighbors into enemies and get a visit from the local sheriff.

There are numerous techniques that can help stop your dog from barking. While all of them can be very successful, you shouldn't expect miraculous results overnight.

Before you try any training techniques, make sure your dog is well-exercised. A dog may be barking out of sheer boredom or because of pent-up energy. Avoid leaving a dog alone for long periods of time.

There are many possible techniques that would be right for your particular pet. Here is an example of a common one: Determine your command phrase for correcting your pooch when he barks. This can be "No Bark" or "Quiet." Whatever you feel comfortable with is fine. When your dog barks, correct him each and every time by using your catch phrase and giving Rover a favorite treat immediately after he stops barking, even for only a second. You must be consistent and correct him each time, as you do not want your dog to get confused as to when he can and cannot bark.

After you give your dog a treat, praise your furry friend for being a good dog and being quiet. Do this each time he barks. Each time you do this with your pooch, wait a few seconds longer after your catch-phrase before giving a treat, holding the treat in front of him. Each time the dog barks, extend the time that he will wait for the treat, while being quiet. Everyone in your family needs to be included in the training, including a pet-sitter.

Whatever technique you use, remember your dog will not be trained overnight. It takes time to break the habit of excessive barking. Keep your training sessions positive and upbeat. Remain calm and patient, and eventually he will bark only when appropriate.

Consult your veterinarian and/or trainer if you continue to face barking issues despite your best efforts.

# Pets grieve, too

In 2011 when Navy SEAL Jon Tumilson, who was killed in Afghanistan, lay in a coffin, draped in an American flag, his loyal Labrador, Hawkeye remained by his casket with his head down for the entire funeral. Hawkeye was in mourning for his beloved companion.

Pets, just like humans, can experience feelings of grief and go through a mourning period when they lose a close companion, whether it's their pet parent or another furry friend in the household.

According to Dr. Sophia Yin, a San Francisco-based veterinarian and animal behaviorist, "Grief is one of the emotions dogs experience, just like people."

The American Society for the Prevention of Cruelty to Animals conducted a Companion Animal Mourning Project in 1996. The study found that

36 percent of dogs ate less than usual after the death of another canine companion. About 11 percent actually stopped eating completely. And around 63 percent of dogs vocalized more than normal or became quieter. More than half the surviving pets became more affectionate and clingy with their pet parents or caregivers. Overall, the study revealed that 66 percent of dogs exhibited four or more behavioral changes after losing a furry companion.

How can you help a dog that is grieving deal with his pain?

Mourning may lead to a loss in appetite, lowered water intake, sluggish response to people and other pets, a loss of interest in play or physical activity, and even a few mournful howls. The symptoms can also increase gradually over weeks or months.

It's also important to know that these changes in behavior can also indicate an illness, so it's important to have an exam done by Rover's veterinarian to be sure that there's not an underlying medical cause.

If you find your furry friend moping around the house after the death of an animal or human family member, the best thing for you to do is to get your dog's mind off the loss by engaging him in fun activities such as a game of fetch, brisk walks and play dates with other pets. The physical interaction promotes a sense of joy and connectedness, and also releases oxytocin, a hormone that increases a sense of well-being and bonding in all mammals.

Provide him with more attention and affection, and if Rover enjoys human company, invite friends that he likes to visit and spend time with him. Another way to keep your dog busy is with food toys. Hide them around the house during the day filled with his favorite treat.

While extremely long periods of grieving aren't normal in dogs, simply showing patience and understanding to your pet in mourning can help an anguished dog cope, suggests anthropologist Elizabeth Marshall Thomas.

Maintaining a normal routine for your dog, such as a familiar eating time or playtime, is the best way to help with the grieving process.

If you are thinking about adding another dog, please wait until you and your furry family member have adjusted to the loss. Forcing Rover to get to know a newcomer may only add stress to his emotional state.

Remember to be patient. Your dog may miss his companion as much as you do.

# Chapter 52

# Is your pet making you sick?

Most pet parents don't need reminding that animals make folks feel good; they are great to have as a family member, and it is well known that people who have pets are typically happier and live longer than those who don't.

But sometimes your furry friend may get sick, and this may leave you wondering if you or your family might be able to catch whatever it is that is making your pet sick.

You can't catch a cold from your dog. But certain illnesses can be spread from pets to humans.

Zoonotic illnesses are diseases humans can get from animals. Many infectious diseases can spread from animals to people, and some of these can come from your furry friend.

Zoonotic diseases can be caused by viruses, bacteria, parasites, and fungi.

Since humans interact with their furry friends on a daily basis, it's important to be aware of the different ways you can get zoonotic diseases. This can include coming into contact with the saliva, blood, urine or feces of an infected pet.

Being aware of the various zoonotic diseases animals can transmit is important, especially when you are a pet parent.

When it comes to pets and parasite, most people think of fleas. Even though they are quite small, it's fairly obvious when your furry friend has them, he starts to scratch, a lot. A lot of pet parents know that fleas are a real nuisance to their dog, and even to family members if your home becomes infested. But most people are unaware that fleas can carry and spread sickness and life-threatening diseases to both pets and people.

Fleas that feed on rats that have typhus travel to pets and feed off them and humans. The feces from these infected fleas can get into your mouth or a wound when you pet your dog.

Thankfully, there are many flea treatments available to help protect your pet and your home.

According to Kerilynne McDowell, DVM, a mobile veterinarian in Sisters, Oregon there have been a few cases of canines with scabies in the last couple of months.

Sarcoptic mange, or "scabies," is also zoonotic and is a highly contagious skin parasite. The mites burrow into the skin and cause severe itching, so dogs that experience prolonged scratching and hair loss are suspect. It is a non-seasonal parasite that can be found in dogs of all ages and breeds.

Maintaining your dog's health is important in preventing scabies. Dogs that roam with other dogs or reside at a shelter or boarding facility are more susceptible to the mite. Scabies is highly contagious to other dogs and humans.

Hookworms and roundworms are intestinal parasites routinely found in dogs, particularly puppies. The worms' eggs are passed from pets through their feces. You can pick them up through your skin from walking barefoot or playing outside. A young child might accidently swallow the eggs by petting an infected animal that licked his anal area and then its coat.

Don't let your infected puppy lick you or your children, and always wash your hands after petting your furry friends.

There is also a zoonotic skin fungus called ringworm. It's not really a worm; it's a fungal infection within the top layer of the skin. It is very contagious, and dogs, cats and other animals can pass ringworm to humans, and humans can also pass it to pets. You can also pick it up from touching surfaces that an infected pet has touched.

Ringworm causes a ring-shaped, reddish rash that may or may not be itchy. See your veterinarian or physician immediately if you or your pet has symptoms. Using a bleach solution, clean all surfaces that you're furry friend came into contact with.

You can reduce the risk of parasitic infection to your family by eliminating parasites from pets: restricting access to contaminated areas, such as sandboxes, pet "walk areas," and other high-traffic areas.

Practicing good hygiene by always washing your hands after handling your pets and maintaining your pets' health is also very important.

Keep current on vaccinations and parasite preventions, keep your furry friends groomed, and get them checked by the veterinarian if they show any signs of illness or if there are any changes.

# SPECIAL SECTION

## Pet Tales to warm the heart:

"When an eighty-five pound mammal licks your tears away, then tries to sit on your lap, it's hard to feel sad."
                    -Kristan Higgins (author, *In Your Dreams*)

We are a nation of dog lovers and there's good reason.

Dogs wait at the door when they know you're coming home and dance with excitement when they see you.

No matter what.

Dogs can reduce stress, anxiety, and depression, ease loneliness, encourage exercise and playfulness, and even improve your cardiovascular health. Caring for a dog can help children grow up more secure and active.

Dogs can provide beneficial companionship for older adults. Perhaps most importantly, a dog can add real joy and unconditional love to your life.

These stories are interesting, funny, sad and real. They are all true stories about man's best friend.

# Cancer survivors thrive together

When Sisters, Oregon resident Jeanie Ogden was diagnosed with breast cancer just over a year ago, she was stunned. Breast cancer didn't even run in her family.

According to www.breastcancer.org, there are about 190,000 new cases of invasive breast cancer and 60,000 cases of non-invasive breast cancer this year in American women.

Just being a woman is the biggest risk-factor for developing breast cancer.

"Everything happened very quickly. After my annual mammogram, I was told that my doctor wanted me right back for a second image. I ended up with a biopsy that day," Ogden said. "I got the results the next day and within a couple of days, I had an appointment for surgery two weeks later to remove the invasive cancer."

Ogden underwent a lumpectomy on her right breast.

"I was very lucky my sentinel lymph nodes were clear and the tumor wasn't that big. It was extremely slow-growing and a non-aggressive cancer," Ogden said.

Ogden needed to follow up with radiation for five weeks following the surgery.

"I was just going to deal with the situation, and so the day after surgery I was out riding my bicycle," Ogden said.

Just about the time Ogden was finishing with her radiation, she noticed that a new family had moved into the neighborhood with a black Labrador retriever.

Ogden had dogs growing up, but decided on cats as she matured. She and her husband Andy are pet parents to two cats that live with them in their comfortable home on Whychus Creek.

The new neighborhood dog was usually outside in the family's yard. Ogden would glance at the good-looking Labrador every now and then as she worked outside, not only because the dog was pretty but because Ogden needed an exercise routine and just maybe, that black Lab did too.

"I finally got up enough nerve to ask the dog's family if I could walk her on a daily basis. I was happy that Jay Jay would be able to join me on my exercise routine," Ogden said. "It was like a new lease on life; I had a wonderful new friend to share my walks on the trail with."

Ogden looked forward to walking Jay Jay every day and it became a therapeutic routine.

"She's all nose and all ears when we're out on the trail. She really channels her inner hunter when we are walking and is oblivious to anything else, including other dogs," Ogden said.

The events that followed seemed more like a serendipitous synchronicity than coincidence.

"One day as Jay Jay and I were walking on the Peterson Ridge trail we met up with Dr. Dana Bailey, a veterinarian at Broken Top Veterinarian Clinic," Ogden explained. "I guess it was by habit, because she checked Jay Jay over for lumps and bumps, and then commented on the obvious lump that was protruding from Jay Jay's chest. She mentioned that I should get it checked out."

Ogden mentioned running into Dr. Bailey to Jay Jay's family.

Her family agreed to take her to Dr. Bailey at Broken Top Veterinary Clinic and found out that the lump was cancerous. It was in early February 2015.

"I felt a sense of urgency for Jay Jay, because when I was diagnosed with breast cancer I had surgery very quickly and I thought that acting rapidly was an important factor in her case," Ogden said.

It was a financial burden for Jay Jay's family to continue with surgery, so Ogden offered to adopt Jay Jay, so she could have the best of care.

"I had wanted to adopt her anyway; we were so bonded after months of walking together," Ogden explained.

"Soon after that, her owner called me on Valentine's Day and said that we could have Jay Jay. It was a heart-wrenching decision that affected both of us. He cared so much for her that he wanted only the best for her.

"Jay Jay had a mast cell tumor. It almost looked like a pink hairless sac hanging off her skin. Her tumor was big and they usually are smaller, like a pimple," Dr. Bailey said. "It was a huge surgery for Jay Jay, but we got the whole thing off and she's doing well with that.

"After surgery Jay Jay was drowsy, but by the next morning she was already up and wagging her tail," Ogden said. "But during surgery to remove the tumor Dr. Bailey noticed a benign mass under her tongue, eosinophilic Granuloma, a hyper response by the immune system, or an immunity problem."

Ogden has Jay Jay on a special diet for that problem. Right now, Jay Jay is cancer-free.

"My life revolves around Jay Jay, and every morning we go for a long walk down the Peterson Ridge trail together. Then another outing during the day and then one walk after dinner. Its great exercise for both of us," Ogden said.

"We also found out that Jay Jay's first family had her trained as a therapy dog and had purchased her as a puppy. That explains why she is so calm and well-behaved. We are actually her third and last family; she has found her forever home with us!"

# Therapy dog helps with crisis intervention team

Dale Coats and his dog Buddy have something in common: they are both trained and certified for the Tri-County School Response (SRT) crisis intervention team.

Coats has over 10 years of experience when it comes to understanding the benefits that therapy dogs can bring into different situations.

"I feel like I'm a pioneer when it comes to expanding an area where therapy dogs can help," said Coats. "We have just scratched the surface as to where these amazing animals can be used." Coats' dog Buddy is a gentle 7-year-old golden retriever that was certified through Therapy Dogs International when he was 2 years old.

"We got Buddy after our dog Lucky passed away in 2006," recalled Coats. "Lucky was also a certified therapy dog."

Therapy dogs are specially trained to offer companionship and comfort. These special canines are brought into hospitals, prisons, schools and disaster areas to provide their unique services to people in need.

In the beginning, Coats started Buddy with Partners in Care.

"His very first call was from a friend whose dad was dying. I brought Buddy over for a visit right away," said Coats. "My friend told me that it was the first time his dad smiled in a long time."

Dale Coats is always taking the initiative to find new areas that therapy dogs can be beneficial.

Three years ago Coats was watching a local news station, listening to the director of Tri-County School Response. He was amazed at the work they were doing in the schools. Tri-County School Response Team is a volunteer effort among specially trained teachers, counselors and community people who are willing to aid schools and community in response to crisis.

The focus of the crisis team is working with schools in the aftermath of student and staff death or other tragedies that overwhelm their usual abilities to cope.

"I decided to call and find out if they had ever used a therapy dog in the past as part of the crisis intervention," Coats said. "They had never used a dog before."

Coats and Buddy both attended 30 hours in the Crisis Management Institute so they could be part of the School Response Team.

"When there's a tragedy in one of our county schools, a team member gets called, and then they bring in our team so we can teach the teachers how to respond," said Coats. "They have a special safe-room, usually the library; that's where Buddy goes and lies down on a blanket."

The safe-room is where students and staff can go if they need a break from the mainstream for a time. The team members assist the staff and students in addressing issues of grief.

Buddy is a team member.

"Kids will usually go right up to Buddy and hug him," said Coats. "They just open up and start talking things out around him; Buddy's presence seems to make it easier for them to cope."

Buddy is the first dog to be certified with the Tri-County-school Response Team for Deschutes, Crook and Jefferson Counties in Oregon.

# English bulldog has rough recuperation

Lola Bean, a 4-year-old English bulldog who has gained fame in numerous walks for charity causes, has recently had major surgery for ACL tears in both legs. Now the Sisters community is reaching out to help with her medical bills.

Lola's claim to fame started with the Feedin' the People Charity Walk in Bend a few years ago. Pet parent Brian Foutz remembers her first walk.

"Lola walked along with my wife, Genny, and I (sic) in the parade with a pink bandana. And another time she had a Wonder Woman cape on. Everyone seems to gravitate toward her, probably because she loves people and they know it," Foutz said.

Then in 2013, Lola, along with her pet parents, started participating in the Walk MS event in Bend, Oregon.

"My aunt Louise, Weese for short, has MS, so we decided to decorate a yard cart that said 'Walking for Weese' and then we dressed Lola up in a knock-off orange tee shirt with iron-ons that also said 'Walking for Weese,'" said Foutz. "People started recognizing her and would look for her at each of the walks."

Lola was also brave enough to participate in a mini ice-bucket challenge last year while sitting in her kiddie pool.

"We made a donation in her name and a video of it," Foutz said. "She didn't mind at all."

Then five months ago, the usually high-spirited Lola Bean began to limp.

"We took her to the vet and at that time she had probably just pulled something, maybe a muscle in her leg. But Lola isn't your typical bulldog, she is very active and loves to jump and play a lot," Foutz said. "She was doing better for a while but started limping again. Then, she decided to jump off the porch instead of going down the few steps, and hit the ground hard."

During the visit to the veterinarian, the Foutzs found out that Lola's ACL was torn in her left leg. She needed surgery. Their vet called Dr. Robert Fuller, an orthopedic surgeon from Sisters, Oregon who is experienced with ACL tears.

The Foutzs think of Lola as a furry family member and refer to her as their "fur baby." For them there was only one decision of how to handle the plight of Lola having a torn ACL. They opted for the surgery.

Then the week before surgery was scheduled Lola tore the ACL in her right leg.

"Lola was using her right leg to compensate for her left," explained Foutz. "We talked to Dr. Fuller and he agreed to do the surgery on both at the same time."

The surgery went well, and the prognosis is hopeful, but with a long recovery time of three months or more.

Lola's recovery hasn't been easy, and last week she had to return to the vet because she couldn't stand up at all.

"Lola has pins inside of her leg that are acting like her ACLs. The mobility in her left leg has a little bit of play in it and her muscle needs to build up again over time," Foutz said. "Dr. Fuller told us she might need up to six months of recuperation, but we are hopeful."

Adopting a dog into the household requires a commitment to his health and well-being. But sometimes with medical emergencies, there are financial hardships.

Brian and Genny Foutz are appreciative of any help they can get for Lola.

"We are hoping to raise awareness that when you have a pet, to remember that anything can happen at any time, just like with people," Foutz said.

# Black Butte beagle thrives in forever home

An ad about a dog was placed in the Sisters, Oregon local newspaper, The Nugget, last March when a hiker found a sweet female beagle on the summit of Black Butte in Sisters. She had no collar and was shaking under a tree. There was fresh snow on the ground and no evidence of other hikers or people up there.

The ad also contained a captivating photo of the beagle that gained popularity among Sisters folks who still would like to know if she has found a good home.

Two months before the ad was placed, Sisters residents Susan and Jim Long lost their beagle, Buddy, when he passed away at 16 years old.

"The timing when the ad in The Nugget came out was serendipitous, because it had been a couple of months after Buddy had died. We really enjoy beagles and have had two in our lives," said Susan Long, Bi-Mart pharmacy technician. "After thinking it over for about a week, I finally called the number in the ad."

Brent, the hiker, brought the beagle over to meet the Longs.

"Brent explained to us that after he finally rescued the beagle on the second attempt, he took her to a vet and she was diagnosed with a broken right hip and had minor frostbite on her paw pads and the tip of her nose," Long said. "She was underweight, and maybe a year old. Her young age must have been a factor in her fast healing. She could have been up on Black Butte for over a week, but nobody knows why she was found there. But none of that mattered to us, because it was love at first sight."

The "sweet female beagle" is now called BB, named after Black Butte, and has adjusted extremely well in her forever home.

"We are very happy with BB," Long said. "And she seems quite happy with us, especially Jim. She tends to be a daddy's girl, and my son Ryan just adores her."

"She's too cute for her own good," said Ryan Long, 2012 Sisters High School graduate. "I get stopped all the time when I take her for a walk, because people like to remark on just how cute she is."

When BB was first found, she weighed in at only 13 pounds, and now she is a healthy 21 pounds.

"We also have a cat, and at first she wanted nothing do with BB, but now they have become the best of friends," said Susan. "They sit together and groom each other!

"I still puzzle over what really happened to her. It's hard to believe all that she went through, because she is such a wonderful dog, and without issues. I believe this was meant to be. BB is so attached to all of us; she is an amazing family member."

# Children benefit from therapy dogs

Relocating to Sisters, Oregon from Tulare County, California, in April was a last-minute deal for Hal and Jennifer Boley and their four dogs.

"We lived in Three Rivers, which is near the entrance to Sequoia National Park, for 30 years, but just couldn't take the heat during the summer anymore. So we were on our way to check out a home in Washington, when my son called and said he was moving to Bend, Oregon, with the grandkids, so we changed direction," said Jennifer Boley. "Since we didn't want to live in the city, we stopped in Sisters and just knew it was the right place for us to settle down."

Two of their four furry family members are certified therapy dogs. Griffyn is a golden retriever and Sham'iran, a great pyrenees.

Boley raised golden retrievers and worked as a veterinarian technician for over 40 years. Her first two golden retrievers, Cody and Wendy, were rescue dogs and when Wendy gave birth to a beautiful litter of puppies, Golden retrievers became an integral part of Boley's life.

"One winter, about 18 years ago, a skier disappeared in the Sequoia National Park, and that motivated me to get into search and rescue with Kara and Larsonary, two of my goldens at the time," said Boley. "We worked with the Tulare County Sheriff Department and the National Park Service."

As Kara aged she went from being active in search and rescue to becoming a therapy dog. Being a therapy dog for the frail and elderly turned out to be Kara's true gift, when one day something magical happened.

"I took Kara to visit patients in skilled nursing facilities, and one day we came across a man who had been in a coma for weeks," Boley said. "The man's father was sitting by his bedside when Kara and I came in to visit. I asked the father if I could help his son pet Kara, by putting my hand on top of his hand. I guided his hand gently over her fur back and forth for a few minutes. The man turned his head toward Kara and opened his eyes; it was his very first voluntary move since the coma! He then started petting Kara on his own. It was a miracle."

Therapy dogs have been used around the globe for years, and there is mounting evidence that dogs truly can heal. A patient's blood pressure drops and heart rate slows, with just one look at a therapy dog strolling into a hospital room.

Boley utilized her golden retrievers as therapy dogs to provide affection and comfort to people in hospitals, retirement homes and hospices, and to people with learning difficulties.

After Griffyn was born six years ago, Boley decided to stop breeding golden retrievers since the shelters were full of unwanted mixed breeds and purebreds.

"I had to keep Griffyn, he was the first born and there was something very special about him, he was just so watchful," said Boley. "When Griffyn was a year old he was tested as a therapy dog with Therapy Dogs International and passed with flying colors."

Boley and Griffyn visited hospice patients in skilled nursing facilities and private homes.

"We had one patient that we visited every week for three years at her home. She was blind but just loved Griffyn, and on her 105th birthday her family invited Griffyn to go with them to an elegant restaurant in which under the special circumstances, he was allowed to go. He sat right beside my chair and had filet mignon," said Boley.

When Griffyn was two years old, Boley adopted a great pyrenees and named him Sham'iran, which is Hebrew for guardian. He is also a certified therapy dog.

Since moving to Sisters just a few short months ago, Griffyn has found his way into the hearts of the children at Camp Sunrise.

Camp Sunrise is a special place for children age 7-14 that have experienced the recent death of a loved one. The camp is open each June to 40 children who reside in Deschutes, Jefferson and Crook counties, and is free of charge. The camp is held at the United Methodist Church camp on Suttle Lake, sponsored by the joint effort of hospice programs.

"Griffyn always seems to have a smile on his face for everyone, and a lot of the kids gravitated toward him at the camp," Boley recalled.

# Therapy dog benefits special-needs students

Nikko, an 8-year-old Collie, uses her calming nature to help students in the life-skills program at Sisters High School.

Her owner, Martha Adamson, knew that one day Nikko would be a good candidate in helping people in need.

"Even as a puppy she had a very calm and loving disposition."

Nikko is certified by Therapy Dogs International. According to TDI, therapy dogs have a long and successful track record as helpers in the areas of mental health, speech and language communication, along with reading support and encouragement. The goal of the therapy dog project is to add one more resource teachers can use to help students achieve to the best of their potential.

Josh Nordell is a special-education teacher who created the life-skills program in Sisters, Oregon four years ago. The class helps special-needs students from fifth grade up to age 21.

"The program focuses on developing skills that students need to become successful adults," said Nordell. "Therapy dogs are beneficial to this program because they give unconditional love no matter what challenges each child has in their life."

"We would arrive each Friday right before the adaptive martial arts class," Adamson said. "Josh scheduled the visits with Nikko as a quiet time for the students."

The name Nikko means sunshine in Japanese.

"The students faces lit up and they become calmer and more focused when Nikko was in the classroom," Adamson said. "They would pet Nikko and talk to him; he really was excited to visit."

After a few visits the students felt really comfortable around Nikko and Adamson began letting them take Nikko outdoors for walks around the school.

"Each of the students had a chance to walk her; I was teaching them some good dog manners," said Adamson. "It helps with their self-esteem; it was really a learning experience about the very basics of dog training, something they might be able to use as a life skill."

Nikko is a happy dog when she is working with children, including at the bereavement program at Camp Sunrise.

Nikko plans to be at Camp Sunrise again this summer wagging her tail, eager to give support to bereaved children in every way she can.

## Therapy dog thrives through hospice program

Hasli, an 8-year-old yellow Labrador retriever, has learned his share of adaptability through exceptional situations as a therapy dog.

His owner, Eloise Barry went through hospice training so she could utilize his lovable disposition for people that request therapy dogs through Hospice of Redmond, located in Central Oregon. Barry renews his certification every two years through Therapy Dogs International.

He has been a therapeutic aid for elderly residents in skilled nursing facilities and has helped the healing process of bereaved children at Sisters' Camp Sunrise in Sisters, Oregon.

Hasli started out as a therapy dog over six years ago visiting Saylor Ennis each week. Ennis passed away two years ago shortly after his 100th birthday.

"He used to tell me he wouldn't know what to do without his good friend Hasli," Barry recalled. "They were so fond of each other."

Therapy dogs have the uncanny ability to help calm and soothe agitated individuals while lifting the spirits of those who are sad and lonely. They provide a medium for physical touch and display affection for those who have lived isolated lives. Therapy dog volunteers and their canines have contributed significantly over the years in bringing warmth and joy to residents of nursing homes.

Barry began taking Hasli to Redmond Health Care, a skilled nursing home, five years ago. They visit residents individually in their rooms and sometimes in a group setting.

"The residents love to pet him and some hug him, they cheer up when they see him coming," Barry said.

Hasli, with his natural desire to please, also visits residents at Clare Bridge in Bend which provides Alzheimer's and dementia care for seniors.

"Our visits are so much fun, the residents love to talk to him," said Barry. "Even the residents that have advanced dementia that sometimes don't respond seem to light up when he comes close by."

Camp Sunrise is a special place for children age 7-14 that have experienced the recent death of a loved one. The camp is open each June to 40 children who reside in Deschutes, Jefferson and Crook counties and is free of charge. The camp is held at the United Methodist Church camp on Suttle Lake, sponsored by the joint effort of hospice programs.

Barry and Hasli have been involved in this powerfully effective weekend each summer for several years.

"We stay there the whole weekend," said Barry. "Hasli loves the children and they enjoy him, they seem to have a special bond together."

Hasli still has a couple more endeavors up his furry sleeve, but Camp Sunrise will remain his priority each year.

# Abused dog becomes a hospice hero

When Jacque Fleming first found Bear, a 7-month-old Australian shepherd, he had a cracked skull; he was a victim of abuse. That was two years ago. Now Bear brings comfort and earns smiles as a therapy dog for elderly hospice patients in Sisters, Oregon.

Fleming was somewhat skeptical when she answered what sounded like a desperate plea - a "Dog needs a home" ad on the Bend-area Craigslist nearly two years ago. Fleming was not new to animal rescue, yet when she arrived at the house to see the dog in the ad, she was deeply saddened.

"It was a bad situation, too many dogs in dirty cages, too many people in a filthy household," said Fleming. She gently lifted the thin, matted dog named Bear out of his cage as he trembled in fear. "I noticed there was a big knot on top of his head," said Fleming. The entire way home in my car, he shook." Fleming's fears were confirmed by her veterinarian. Bear had a cracked skull. The dog's physical injury would heal with time, but would his emotional ones?

Because Fleming is an old-fashioned farm girl, Bear was welcomed to a new home of over 150 acres, with four horses, chickens, two rescue dogs and a cat.

"That first year, Bear would run and hide when friends would visit. He was especially fearful of men," recalled Fleming. "I decided the best therapy for Bear would be to bring him everywhere with me, including work."

Fleming is a hospice caregiver for the frail and elderly in Sisters. Time does heal emotional wounds; Bear has become a healing tool for her elderly clients.

One such client is Ethel Lindsay of Sisters.

"She is 95 years old and appreciates Bear, since pets had always been part of her life; he sits by her every day we come by," said Fleming. "I take Ethel to get a hamburger every Friday; she always makes sure that Bear gets one, too.

"The patients respond to his gentle touch; he seems to understand their needs," said Fleming. "Hospice patients have asked for Bear to be with them at the end."

Fleming has a huge heart for all animals, especially those that need that extra care.

"I once rescued a baby buffalo; she was born premature and had lost her mom," said Fleming. "They weren't going to give her a chance, so I did."

The buffalo lived and has had calves of her own. She also rescued a blind llama.

# SAR dog gains experience

Training to be a SAR volunteer for the Camp Sherman Hasty Team in Sisters, Oregon is a big commitment. You need to be comfortable with the outdoors and possess the time and willingness to serve the public.

For Jacobus Von Logan, or just plain "Jake," it's been second nature.

Jake, a 6-year-old Dutch/German shepherd mix has been part of the Camp Sherman Hasty SAR team for four years. His owner and handler, Mark Hilgart is also a team member.

Jake was trained as a search and rescue dog, and was ready for the team by the time he was 2 years old.

Jake completed foundation obedience classes at advanced levels before he could begin SAR training.

Jake was trained to be a trailing search and rescue dog. A trailing dog works on leash and follows the scent path of the subject, not the track.

"Jake and I have been called in on four search and rescues over the last few years," recalls Hilgart.

"Two years ago there was a search and rescue over in John Day Canyon located in Eastern Oregon. Two hikers were lost. First they searched for them by plane and had people looking on foot for hours, but weren't successful. Then at 9 p.m. they called in our SAR team. We started with a briefing about the situation and Jake got to sniff the scent of the hikers from something that belonged to them. I use a sterile pad on clothing or shoes of the missing person, then give Jake the scent, I find it works the best. An hour or so later Jake had picked up on their scent and we called in on our radio to give the deputy our position. Then the planes came in and spotted the two missing men."

Hilgart and Jake have been trained for high mountain rescue in rough terrain. But they never track alone.

"There are several key people with us on each search and rescue mission. We have about 30 volunteers who go through 140 hours of training on our Camp Sherman Hasty Team. It could be someone with advanced medical training like an EMT or a marathoner runner that helps us track," said Hilgart. "Since I am Jake's handler, I need to focus on him because he shows me what to do and I don't want to break his concentration. Another volunteer will be using the radio to call in and so on."

Jake wears a tracking harness and has several different kinds of leads depending on the situation.

"On the harness is a pack in which I carry essential tools that can be very useful. I have a search and rescue whistle, a GPS for giving a position, and a compass. I also have bright polka-dot tape for marking areas and a headlamp for nighttime use. Jake really loves his important role as a SAR dog," says Hilgart.

Jefferson County Deputy Dave Blann has been coordinator of the Camp Sherman Hasty Team for the last 18 years.

"The whole team is made up of people from all walks of life. They each bring their own talents to the team and let us utilize that talent," says Blann.

"Jake is an excellent tool to have in your tool box and his handler Mark Hilgart has put forth thousands of hours working with him. It's amazing what those two have done for our SAR team."

Hilgart and his wife have adopted another Dutch/German shepherd named Zoe. She is a year old.

"She has already been through all her obedience training and will be following in Jakes footsteps as a search and rescue dog in the near future," says Hilgart. "Jake will be retiring in another two years."

Hilgart will begin training Zoe as a trailing search and rescue dog in about a month.

"Even as a puppy I would roll the ball instead of throwing it so Zoe would keep her nose to the ground. We play hide and seek for her to practice tracking," says Hilgart. "Jake is her mentor, she learns quickly by watching him."

Hilgart and his wife live in Sisters, Oregon at their Lucky Star Ranch with their miniature horses, miniature donkeys, and Jake and Zoe.

# Local couple adopts another rescue dog

Sometime last fall a three- to four-month-old black German shepherd mix dog was found roaming the streets of Yakima, Washington. He had no tags or microchip. Luckily for this homeless pup, someone picked him up and brought him to Wags to Riches Animal Rescue and Sanctuary near Yakima.

Sisters, Oregon resident Wendy Holzman and her husband, Alan, have faced the challenges of adopting a shelter dog more than once, and when they saw the sweet face of the black shepherd mix puppy on Petfinder they decided to meet him.

"Our daughter Maya was home for Christmas and I had mentioned that we were thinking about getting another dog. It's been over a year that our dog Sadie passed away," said Wendy.

When they adopted Sadie from Heartland Humane Society in Corvallis 12 years ago, she was a headstrong seven-month-old black and white Border collie mix that loved people.

"My daughter and I started looking on Petfinder. We found out that the animal rescue organization kept the puppy that was found wandering in Yakima for about a month to see if someone would claim him, but nobody did," Holzman said.

"Then he went to foster care, and that's where we adopted him from. By then he was already over five months old and very healthy. We brought him home on January 3, right after the new year, and named him Colby.

"We had a honeymoon period with Colby where things were great. And then it was couple of rough months, so we turned to dog trainer Anne Geser."

According to the ASPCA, most newly adopted dogs are in a state of severe adjustment to what is a whole new world for them. It's a new environment, with new sights, sounds, people and possibly other animals, and can result with a dog sort of shutting down as he absorbs all of this new information and tries to figure out his place in his new world. Think of it like a human being plopped down in a new country. The new dog seems fairly calm, passive, and quiet, but as he becomes adjusted and more comfortable his true personality shines through. Many people end up calling a dog trainer for help after weeks have passed with their new dog.

The behaviors aren't really new to the dog; they just seem new to the dog to his pet parents. So when these behaviors start to show themselves, people are often caught off guard.

"I remember Colby trying to bite our feet while we were walking," said Alan Holzman. "And when we were sitting down eating dinner he would jump right into our lap! He didn't understand what we wanted from him."

"We worked with Ann Geser, and she really helped us understand more about Colby and his behaviors," Wendy said. "Without her help I don't know what we would have done; she did a wonderful job and we learned clicker training. He was in a negative behavior pattern and he needed positive reinforcement. Colby has now turned a corner to where everything is fitting into place. It's been fun watching him really come around, he's a great dog."

Colby goes to Central Bark for daycare once a week, and will be going to group lessons at Dancin' Woofs in Bend.

"We had one private lesson with Kristin, owner of Dancin' Woofs, and she recommended a harness for Colby since he was never leash trained, and that's what we're working on. One thing about Colby is that he plays nicely with other dogs," said Wendy Holzman.

"Colby now has a much better idea of what we want from him, and he's a wonderful part of our family."

# Woman injured by off-leash dog

It started out as a wonderful September day for retired Sisters, Oregon resident Jo Reitan and her seven-year-old standard poodle, Kari. They were enjoying each other's company on one of their daily strolls down the walking path in Tollgate, with Kari on leash.

What was about to happen would change Reitan's life in a way she never would have expected.

During their walk, Reitan noticed a man, a woman and a large unleashed dog standing in a driveway around 50 feet away. Instinctively Reitan turned with Kari to walk away from the unleashed dog, just in case he might notice Kari and get distracted.

"Kari and I headed in the opposite direction hoping the dog wouldn't see us," Reitan said. "Less than one minute and bang, the dog was right behind us and grabbed a hold of Kari's tail. The next thing I knew the dog was in my face and I was on the ground and in pain, it happened that fast. The dog didn't seem aggressive; he just wasn't under anyone's control."

While bites and maulings are the most common form of injuries caused by dogs, there are additional accidents responsible for thousands of injuries each year in the United States. They include knock-downs, tripping and falling over dogs, and even head-butts. In an excitable state, a dog can jump up on you and knock you down. Non-aggressive dogs sometimes unintentionally trip or knock people down, resulting in injuries.

"I yelled for the man and woman to come over," Reitan said. "When they did I asked them to go over to my neighbor Robert Kempvanee's house nearby, because he is a retired fire chief and a friend of mine. The man and woman didn't seem to know what to do, but they did grab the collar of the dog and walk off. Then a woman in a van came by and asked if I needed help and she went and to get Robert or somebody did. It's hard to be sure since so many nice people stopped and asked if they could help.

"When Robert came to help me, he took Kari home, who was really shook up, and he decided to take me to the emergency room in my small car because I couldn't get up and it was easier to get me into a smaller vehicle, rather than his truck."

Non-aggressive dog accidents are responsible for thousand of trips each year to emergency rooms around the country.

"The hospital directed us to the orthopedic center, and I was seen by Michael Caravelli, MD, an orthopedic surgeon. After an X-ray, the surgeon told me that it didn't look good, that the fall had forced the femur down into my knee and onto the plateau of the tibia, and they would have to do surgery. It was Thursday, and I stayed in the hospital and had surgery on Saturday.

"My neighbor and friend Pat Rinehart and her partner, Wanda, took care of Kari while I was in the hospital. I contacted the Deschutes County Sheriff's office about the incident and a sheriff actually came to the hospital so I could fill out a report."

Deschutes County has an "at-large" ordinance. According to Deschutes County Animal Control, County Code 6.08.15 defines "at-large" to mean a dog or other animal found off the premise of the owner or keeper while the dog or animal is not under the complete control of a capable person. This would allow for dogs which are trained to be off the leash, however would require them to be under the complete control of the handler.

Failing to control a dog is an act of negligence, even before the dog causes an injury.

The accident has Reitan laid up.

"The surgery turned out good as far as we know right now. I return in four week to see my orthopedic surgeon for a radiograph to see how it's mending," Reitan said. "The entire healing process is 11 weeks, and that's just for me to be able to put weight on my knee."

The Deschutes County Sheriff's Office cited the woman who was the caretaker of the young man who was present at the time of the incident. The owner was not present.

Reitan appreciates all the help she has received in coping with an unexpected injury.

"I've been so lucky all through this because of the Tollgate community effort," Reitan said. "My friends and neighbors have been helping me. My neighbors Tom and Barb Harris have been taking care of me and walking Kari every day. My good friend Robert and his wife Janie have helped so much, too. They cook and clean for me and take good care of Kari while I'm off my knee. My grown kids have been here helping also. My daughter from Tucson, Arizona, Kristi came and helped for nine days. And my son, Shannon and his wife Gaia from Idaho came for a few days to help also."

It's a lot of effort and a lot of disruption - all caused by a moment of inattentiveness that left a dog out of control.

# Mini poodle rescues furry companion

Sisters, Oregon resident and Rotarian Gayla Nelson spends a lot of her time outdoors on her 10-acre ranch, caring for her four horses. Her two dogs - Louie, a 22-pound mini poodle, and Zoe, a tiny Yorkshire terrier - enjoy tagging along. Last month, a routine morning of tending to a horse in need turned into a terrifying ordeal for Nelson and her two furry friends.

"Suddenly I heard Louie start barking like crazy and then I heard Zoe, she was yelping loudly. Then Louie's bark turned vicious and he sounded like a Rottweiler. This all happened within a couple of seconds," Nelson said. "I ran toward them, they weren't far away, and Zoe came limping toward me yelping in pain with blood all over her."

A large coyote had wandered into the yard in broad daylight and nabbed Zoe, the smallest canine. But to the coyote's surprise, Louie became extremely aggressive in protection of Zoe. The coyote was intimidated and dropped Zoe out of the clutches of its sharp teeth.

Coyotes, an icon of the American West, are common in Oregon, where they are widely distributed across the landscape. Coyotes are commonplace in rural areas around Sisters Country, but have been spotted in urban areas as well.

According to Oregon Department of Fish and Wildlife (ODFW), Coyotes are skilled hunters and will eat rodents, birds, snakes, small deer and antelope, insects, fruits and berries. They are opportunistic feeders and will also eat pets, pet food, and garbage.

Coyote conflicts can range from sightings to pet killings to an exceptionally rare attack on a human being. They have been known to attack a family pet in broad daylight, and also domestic livestock.

According to ODFW the key to responding appropriately to a threatening encounter with a coyote is to scare it away. You can shout, bang pots and pans, stomp your feet or wave your arms.

"I couldn't believe it, Louie - who used to be afraid of his own shadow - fearlessly chased that coyote out of the yard," Nelson said. "I kept screaming for Louie to come, and he always listens, but this time he wanted to make sure that the coyote was gone."

Zoe was bleeding with one deep puncture wound by her right shoulder and two on the other shoulder.

"I rushed Zoe to Sisters Veterinary Clinic, and Dr. Pittman attended to Zoe's wounds right away. Zoe had to stay at the vet's all day, but they let her come home at night," Nelson said. "It was a critical period for her. She was on medications and I sat with her all night in my arms. She's been such a close companion to me for six years."

Nelson remembered four years earlier when she rescued Louie from an abusive situation.

"He was frightened of everyone. So I started socializing him by bringing him along on overnight camping excursions with the Ochoco Outlaws, a group of women that ride and camp together, and over time he adjusted really well," said Nelson. "Louie loves going everywhere with me, including when I work with the Oregon Equestrian Trail group, and the Oregon National Guard Youth Corps helps us with trail building. Everyone loves Louie, and he's the only dog allowed out on the work parties."

Zoe is doing great and her wounds have healed well.

"About a week after Zoe's incident with the coyote when I was with my camping group, the women had heard about how fearless Louie was, and they had a naming ceremony," said Nelson. "They made a big production out of what a hero Louie was, and gifted him with a special collar that says "Brave Heart," with a purple feather."

Oregon Department of Fish and Wildlife offers the following tips to help prevent coyote/pet confrontations: Feed pets indoors and do not leave pet food or water bowls outside. Supervise your pets when they are outside; if possible, keep them leashed. If you spot a coyote, keep your distance, have your dog leashed or get him inside as quickly if possible. Do not leave cats or small dogs out after dark. Also, secure your garbage cans in an area inaccessible to wild animals; they can attract coyotes.

# Dog rescued in Camp Sherman finds forever home

Bend, Oregon resident Cindy Wright went through a major life change five years ago when her sister Lori "Woody" Blaylock was murdered. She was overwhelmed by grief and resigned from her job. Wright had no idea where her life was headed.

"I spent time traveling over the last few years deciding what it is I want to do with my life," she recalled. "Since I've always loved animals and had free time, I thought I could try to find local animals that were missing, a little help for someone who is out making a living and not able to search for their lost pet."

Wright had past experience working with animals. When she was younger she was a certified dog groomer and later in life worked as veterinary technician for a short period of time.

"I started out looking for lost animals by volunteering for High Desert Wildlife Rescue & Rehabilitation. And then I was scouring the ads for lost animals on the Pets Lost Bend Oregon Facebook site.

"In September a friend of mine in Bend called and asked me if I had seen a notification for a missing Australian shepherd in the Camp Sherman area," Wright said.

Camp Sherman is an unincorporated community in Jefferson County, Oregon. The Camp Sherman Campground is nestled on the banks of the scenic Metolius River in Deschutes National Forest.

Wright's friend Lisa first saw the notification on the Camp Sherman Store Facebook page on September 28, 2015. Roger White, Camp Sherman Store owner, had posted that they were on a doggie rescue mission for a mid-sized Australian shepherd that had been hanging around the store for approximately two weeks. He mentioned that the dog was very fast and nobody had been able to catch him/her, and left the contact number for the store. White was very concerned because the temperatures had dropped into the 20s at night.

"Numerous people on the staff had been feeding him, but he was so skittish. That dog had been seen all the way down by the fish hatchery and at the Jack Creek campground," White said. "It's amazing that the dog has survived. This is cougar, bear, coyote and elk territory."

Wright never saw the notice about the missing shepherd, but was interested.

"I called the store and talked to one of the staff and told them I would be there in the morning. I didn't mind going the distance because I enjoy photography and the Metolius River area."

Wright brought all her "training things" that would help with the dog's rescue.

"I brought a dog crate, whistles and toys," she said. "It's easier to catch a dog with another dog, but I couldn't find a friend with a dog that could go. And my two at home are elderly."

In the morning the staff at the Camp Sherman Store told Wright that the lost dog would most likely show up, especially since they had started feeding him the week before. Wright started walking down the trail by the store. Another couple was close behind Wright with their older golden retriever, and Wright informed them about the missing dog.

"I asked the couple to let me know if they spotted the dog, and they went on the trail ahead of me. Then another woman with a border collie came running up the trail saying the Australian shepherd dog was close by," Wright explained.

It became a community effort.

"Sure enough the missing dog was down the trail. The Australian shepherd was near the couple with the golden retriever. He seemed to like their dog, Ruby. We sat there for a while and the lost dog kept coming closer and closer. We tried to put a leash around him, but he'd run off. The couple and their dog finally left and I walked back up to the store and the Australian shepherd followed."

Wright asked if the staff could bring out some food to keep him around. And they did.

"I went back to my vehicle and got my own kibble out and slowly moved around to the front of the store where the dog was. I started throwing out food and after only five minutes he was eating out of my hand," Wright said. "After 15 minutes I could pet him while he was eating out of my hand, but would pull away when he thought I was going to touch him."

Wright was running out of food fast. The dog would high-tail it out of there without a fast plan of action.

"I had to grab him by the nape of the neck, and went around underneath to pet him. He tried to bite me, but didn't draw blood," Wright said. "And as soon as I had a good grip on him I asked a gentleman that had parked next to me if he could help get the leash around him. The gentleman obliged, and I had myself a very scared lost dog. I couldn't have done it without the help of so many people."

Wright took the dog to a veterinarian in Tumalo.

"He had no microchip," she said. "I called all of the shelters in the region, but no one knew anything about him being missing. I also had him neutered."

Wright couldn't help naming the little lost dog.

"I named him Jasper, like the gemstone, since its part of his coloring," she said.

He is a purebred miniature Australian shepherd, and its possible Jasper could have been from a puppy mill.

Wright and her 21-year-old daughter, Miryssa, decided that Jasper has found his forever home as part of their family.

"We are socializing and clicker-training him. We are also crate-training Jasper as he has severe separation anxiety. We are slowly getting him used to things," Wright said.

"We have estimated his age between 3 and 5 years old. But to us, he is 5 years old because that's how long my sister has been gone. He gets along great with my other two dogs and loves Miryssa."

# Crisis response canines train in Sisters

Dogs can help people get through a crisis.

Sue Dolezal, controller for Sisters Eagle Airport, her husband Gary, and their dogs Isaac and Foster, are specially trained and certified with National Crisis Response Canines to do just that.

Last October 2, they were deployed to Roseburg to attend the Roseburg candlelight vigil just one day after the UCC shooting.

National Crisis Response Canines held a rigorous three-day training and evaluation in Sisters, Oregon last weekend to recertify teams. Participants arrived from Florida, Alaska, Michigan, Washington and Oregon.

National provides certification for crisis response canine teams who demonstrate competency in working in the complex physical and emotional environments of disaster.

Dogs helping people.

A crisis can be a home fire, domestic violence, child abuse, tragic death, school shooting, missing elder or a crime. A disaster such as wildfires, terrorism or floods can affect an enormous number of people psychologically.

Crisis response canines are specially trained in psychological first aid and certified to work effectively to deal with a person that feels overwhelmed by personal crisis. When someone is hurting, crisis response teams help replace the feeling of fear, anxiety and hopelessness with feelings of being safe, cared for, and capable. The crisis response team works alongside community agencies such as the Red Cross that provide support and assistance.

Sue and Gary Dolezal's dogs are certified crisis response canines, and they used the training last weekend to cross-train their dogs between each other.

"You never know which dog is going to be with whom, so it was something we needed to do," Dolezal said.

Twelve-year-old Henry was certified for crisis response in 2008, and is now retired after eight years of service.

In 2004 Dolezal and her husband got involved with Deschutes County Search and Rescue (SAR).

"I backed off when I started working at the airport, plus I wanted to work more with our dog Henry to get him certified with the crisis response team. Gary has been with SAR for over 10 years and is the logistics chief," said Dolezal.

While dogs in both crisis response and animal-assisted therapy essentially provide the same service - bringing a sense of comfort and safety - the biggest difference is the environment in which they work. Crisis response canines receive advanced training to work in the complex physical environments of disasters and to safely interact with strangers experiencing intense emotions in the aftermath of crisis.

National President Connie Jantzen flew in from Florida to help with instruction and evaluation along with Barbara Geno, a National instructor from Michigan.

"With crisis response work, there's nothing normal," Jantzen says. "You don't know when you're going, the dogs are working in unfamiliar surroundings and the surroundings may be damaged. The dogs have to be able to understand those intense emotions and bring them back to a feeling of calm."

Jantzen's German shepherd, Lady, was the catalyst for her involvement with crisis response canines.

"Lady is now retired from the crisis response team after being of service for about seven years," Jantzen said. "She was a rescue along with her sister, Koda. They were abandoned. The family moved and left them behind in the garage for about three months. I adopted both of them, and Lady was the one that had the affiliation with people, she's been amazing.

"That's what we are looking for in the individual dog, one that has a specific temperament, a dog that is drawn to people and want(s) to be of service to them. The canine needs to be clear-headed and calm when people are in crisis."

Jantzen emphasizes that situations don't need to be disasters or crises in order for the dogs to respond. They'll work with at-risk families or crime victims.

"There's crisis everywhere, whether it's a natural disaster, man-made disaster, or maybe just the death of a loved one," she said.

"Our approach to crisis canine work is to be involved with the community, at the community level. Of course we respond to big disasters, but there are so many things going on every day in our own communities where canines can be of service. We have the trainings in the communities so people can understand where their local resources are and where their local needs are so they can match up those resources with those needs in times of crisis and disaster."

Sisters has a tremendous resource within its community. If something major happened the local crisis response canine team would come in, and then all of the national teams would be deployed here to help the community cope.

On Saturday morning as part of the physical training, the crisis response canine team consisting of five dogs and their handlers, along with evaluators, were invited to show up at the Sisters training ground, where Sisters-Camp Sherman Fire District and Cloverdale Rural Fire Protection District train.

Captain Michael Valoppi was on hand to assist with the crisis response canine team.

Two firefighters had on self-contained breathing apparatus (SCBA) packs, ready to interact with the dogs.

"We want the dogs to be exposed to all the sights and sounds and smells of the firefighters in their turnout gear," said Jantzen. "Because of their masks and respirators, they don't look or smell human anymore. We want to familiarize the dogs to the firefighters, so they understand that under that gear they are still people and they still need to work with them during disaster."

"We are building their confidence before we increase exposure to anything they may or may not be comfortable with during a disaster," added Geno.

For more information about National Crisis Response Canines, visit www. crisisresponsecanines.org.

Edwards Brothers Malloy
Oxnard, CA  USA
January 14, 2016